D1175675

DATE DUE

Hawthorne's View
of the Artist

MILLICENT BELL

HAWTHORNE'S VIEW
OF THE ARTIST

STATE UNIVERSITY OF NEW YORK

Copyright © 1962 by the State University of New York.

All rights reserved.

For information, please write to University Publishers Inc., 239 Park Avenue South, New York 3, N. Y., sole distributors of this book.

Library of Congress Catalog Card Number: 62-13566

Printed in the United States of America

PS
888
B4

To GENE

Preface

~~~~~~

An artist's view of artists is of intimate importance for the rest of humanity. If he succeeds in explaining the nature of his own activities—their aim and their fruit, their gratification and their cost—he tells us more than another might about the conception men generally hold of themselves in his time, and of the relation in his society between the individual and the social, the unique and the characteristic, the intellectual and the practical powers. Perhaps an artist's "portrait of the artist" will be, as the ambiguous phrase suggests, a self-portrait, with lineaments of joy and anguish very like his own. But it is apt to be a portrait not only of himself as artist but as *man*—intellectual or craftsman, idealist or careerist—as he finds himself cast in more common roles, and as he considers their relation to social life. Thus, the artist passes judgment, through this portrait, upon those general human impulses which twine themselves about his unique creative emotions.

How did Nathaniel Hawthorne define the artist, analyze the artist's relations with other men, justify the artist's works? In his personal history there is sufficient evidence that Hawthorne came to ponder deeply the fate first glimpsed when he asked his mother: "What do you think of my becoming an author, and relying for support upon my pen?" In his fiction the subject is pervasive and significant. Yet if one attempts to abstract Hawthorne's conception of artistic function from the rest of his thinking, one realizes at once by what reticular bonds such a man's ideas hold together. The choice of vocation for one who proposes to earn his living through art turns out to be a matter deeply involved with his vision of the moral life. It is intimately engaged with his determinations of the real and the illusional. In plucking forth Hawthorne's views about his profession, one beholds, grasped by tentacular roots, the substance of his thought on related subjects—not the destiny of artists only, but that of all kinds of creative intelligence; not alone the status of the mind-worker, but the conditions imposed upon all singularity or self-development. And as one inquires further one is confronted by still larger questions; it is necessary to consider what Hawthorne's concepts of character—not just the artist's but anybody's—were.

The artist himself appears in major or minor roles throughout Hawthorne's fiction. In "The Artist of the Beautiful," "The Prophetic Pictures," and "Drowne's Wooden Image," he is the special subject of interest. But artists also appear in many other places. Miles Coverdale, the narrator of *The Blithedale Romance,* is a poet; Holgrave, in *The House of the Seven Gables,* is a photographer and a writer; *The Marble Faun* is entirely peopled by inhabitants of the American art colony in Rome, three of the four chief characters being artists; and even Hawthorne's youthful work *Fanshawe* contains at least one poet. A poet plays a part in "The Great Stone Face," in "The Great Carbuncle," and in "The Canterbury Pilgrims," and a good number of Hawthorne's sketches figure an authorial artist-character—Oberon, in the "Fragments from the Journal of a Solitary Man" and "The Devil in Manuscript," the related personality of the narrator of "The Seven Vagabonds" and "Passages from a Relinquished Work," the author-character in "Little Annie's Ramble," "The Village Uncle," and "Graves and Goblins," and, probably, the "I" of "Sights from a Steeple" and "Sunday at Home."

But the results of Hawthorne's interest in the peculiar problem of the artist may not end here. Thomas Mann once remarked that in addition to the tales which express his own interest in the subject of art and the artist—one of Mann's most personal themes—his novel *Royal Highness,* concerned with the life of a prince, "is also an allegory of the life of the artist," and *Felix Krull,* the biography of a criminal, "is in essence the story of an artist," and so also with other stories whose action ostensibly concerns non-artists. I feel that a similar situation may exist in Hawthorne's fiction and that we must look behind the false costumes of quite a number of Hawthorne's characters for the image of the artist.

Hawthorne seems to have felt the identity of the artist's situation with that of many other persons, whose fates may be seen as images of his, as his is of theirs. The variety of the artist's likenesses is indicated, perhaps, in the remark in "The Artist of the Beautiful," that all those "whose pursuits are insulated from the common business of life" are likely to endure the lonely fate of Owen Warland. "What the prophet, the poet, the reformer, the criminal, or any other man with human yearnings, but separated from the multitude by a peculiar lot, might feel, poor Owen felt." We can take this to mean that Hawthorne identified the artist as another of the outcasts of life whose general tragedy interested him so much. Like all great writers, Hawthorne was interested in *human* problems; even his studies of artists are, ultimately, but examples of his convictions concerning sin and redemption, tragedy and happiness. The artist was, to Hawthorne, primarily a man, susceptible to certain temptations and a certain fate common to many men.

Not only in the nature of their destinies, but in the personal qualities that distinguish them from the generality of man, the nonartists of Hawthorne's fiction often display an unmistakable relationship to his artists. It may be said that Hawthorne's group of portraits of the artist is surrounded by a larger number of representations of the artist in some other guise, or, more correctly, by figures that represent some aspect of the artist's personality—his abnormal acuteness concerning human behavior, his impersonality, his devotion to a single object, his receptiveness to sensory beauty, his membership in both the ideal and actual worlds, as well as his "difference" and isolation from other men. F. O. Matthiessen called the heroes of each of Hawthorne's novels "refractions of the artistic nature." Coverdale is, of course, a poet, Kenyon a sculptor, and Holgrave not only a photographer, but a short-story writer, like his creator; Dimmesdale, on the other hand, is a scholarly theologian, whose only expressive "art" is the sermon. Yet it is quite true that Dimmesdale's personality gives some evidence of Hawthorne's thought concerning the artist, for it is an example of the artistic temperament, with some of the fallibilities assigned to it by Hawthorne. We shall find still other such "refractions" in Aylmer of "The Birthmark" and in Clifford Pyncheon. Of course, it cannot be maintained with certainty that in such instances Hawthorne was writing deliberate allegories of the artist's life, as Mann did in *Royal Highness* and *Felix Krull*. Yet the evidence of these stories confirms what we learn from the stories about actual artists.

Hence it is that, as I have developed this study, I have been aware that I was pursuing no easily confined subject, but was searching along the spreading fibers of Hawthorne's most fundamental thought and confronting his art in its indivisible complexity. What I believe has resulted—as much by necessity as intention—is a book about Hawthorne rather than about a "theme," although the theme in question has, indeed, led into many aspects of his creative achievement, helping me to see them in new ways.

Anyone who would write thus largely of Hawthorne is, of course, indebted to the rich series of general critiques he has inspired from Henry James' time to our own. While my notes record only especially significant points of agreement or difference, a large measure of admiring agreement must be assumed in the case of a number of modern commentators—particularly F. O. Matthiessen, Newton Arvin, Randall Stewart, Richard H. Fogle, and Hyatt H. Waggoner.

MILLICENT BELL

Brown University
Providence, Rhode Island

Contents

Hawthorne's View
of the Artist

Chapter I

Introduction:

The Artist as Man

~~~~~~

THE IMPRINT OF FACT

Hawthorne was a man who lived alertly in both the world of events and the world of ideas, and his image of the artist took its form not only from the ideal conceptions of philosophy and art but from diverse models in real life. His view of the artist was also inseparable from his thoughts—the fruit, again, of both practical observation and abstract supposition—about the creative intellect in all its varieties of expression. Perhaps the difficulty of reconciling such a combination of suggestions produced in Hawthorne's fictional descriptions of the artist their poignant complexity, their mixture of the exalted and the mundane, the mythic and the satiric. The difficulty of the task may, indeed, account for the depth and interest of Hawthorne's picture, one in which some of the contradictions between prescription and experience remain unresolved. Hawthorne's was, I believe, the most profound definition of the artist achieved by anyone writing in his time.

As the artist was a man among living men, his activities were, most obviously, definable in terms of the prevailing patterns of social behavior, for which the somewhat tired term "individualism" has long served. What kind of "nine-teenth-century individualist" was the artist of Hawthorne's day? And how did his peculiar abilities of perception and creation, his aim, and mode of achievement, relate to the personality and lives of other kinds of intellectuals and of men generally? As the artist was a mythic or symbolic figure conjured forth by philosophy and by the traditions of art itself, his activities proposed different kinds of identifica-tion, however. How well could the language of current ideas—loosely termed "Romanticism" today—express Haw-thorne's visionary sense of the meaning of the artist? I shall examine these two contexts, the practical and the theoretic, as they seem to me to have been significant to Hawthorne, before turning to close study of the artist-hero evoked in his fiction. Though I speak of the two separately it is certainly self-evident that in Hawthorne's mind there was no such neat separation. Rather, the two elements are compounded, or one is filtered by the other, in a testing of the times by the available theories of life and a testing of the theories by experience.

What did Hawthorne make of the life of his fellow Americans, of the centrifugal, yet "individualistic" nine-teenth century, which had begun to enforce mass standards with increasing firmness upon the average person at the same time—at the very same time—that it gave an unprec-edented range to the expression of those single wills power-ful enough to seize the levers of authority? It has often been pointed out that Hawthorne's most persistent single theme is the peril of egotism. It has been less obvious that this makes him largely a critic of *social* individualism, which is symbolized in the private ego by the trait of pride without sympathy, or self-enhancement achieved at the expense of brotherhood. As Randall Stewart has shown, Hawthorne was often a sharp critic of society, his fiction as well as his note-books reflecting his clear-eyed judgment of contemporary institutions and issues.[1] But in addition to direct comment upon the social scene (as, for example, in *The Blithedale Romance*) and in addition as well to satirical allegorizing of contemporary habits of thought and action (as in "The Celestial Railroad"), we find more pervasive evidence of Hawthorne's social judgment. In his deepest fictional symbols, those often transposed in time and place from all contemporaneity and making no direct reference to popular issues, we can discover symbolic representations of immediate social reality. So, we will see, Hawthorne's criticism of spiritual self-centeredness applies itself to the practical problems of his day. Hawthorne's antagonism toward the Romantic-idealist exaltation of the ego had deep rooting in a distrust of the effects of the free play of economic and social force. While he was drawing his pictures of self-assertion at work in personal relationships, post-Jacksonian America was demonstrating that the democratic scheme was capable of producing on the one hand the all-engorging personality of the fortune-builder or the party boss, and on the other a faceless, bewildered, *un*-individualized industrial population, the "people" degraded into the mass—as Arthur Schlesinger, Jr. has expressed it, "bound together not by common loyalties and aspirations but by common anxieties and fears."[2]

As we examine the special problems of the artist which are analyzed in Hawthorne's fiction, we will note how each can be related to the more general human problems that are the fundamental preoccupation of Hawthorne's writing —and that these have in turn broad contemporary meaning. Egotism, solitariness, a perverse relation to the normal or natural in man and the universe—these hazards of the artistic occupation are dangers for any sort of intellectual. The scientist, the speculative philosopher, the idealist, the reformer—each must bear the burden of gifts of mind which may work harm to himself and others. Most often,

Hawthorne sees such harm as the consequence of mono-mania, of willful separation of the human from the abstract result. But society at large, in Hawthorne's time, was working just such a separation. The guilt complex of the in-tellectual has not been reserved for the atomic scientist; even in the "golden day" it was apparent to many thought-ful men that mere intellectual ability could either be used with a new, vastly extended harmfulness, or it could be trivial, irrelevant, eccentric.

Let us anticipate some of the argument to follow and look at two illustrations of this—two intellectual excesses which receive attention in Hawthorne's fiction, and which seem to have demonic counterparts in the abnormalities of external life in his time. We shall have occasion to consider the perfectionism of the Romantic artist and thinker as a theme of great interest to Hawthorne. Yet with how large a design this theme connects! What else is the all-consuming obsessive principle which built the railroad empires, what else is economic monopoly itself (which first appears in this period) but a sort of perfectionism, admitting no com-petitive exception, tolerating no flaw in the market? It is a far cry from Aylmer, the hero of "The Birthmark," to Cornelius Vanderbilt, yet perhaps not so far as might be supposed. The Romantic quest for unattainable perfection and the prospector's fanatic perseverance were to become curiously linked in the American mind. Already the union of American idealism with the nation's material aspiration had begun to be felt; after the Civil War the streams, as Van Wyck Brooks has observed, flowed together, and "into this one channel passed all the religious fervor of the race." The hero of Mark Twain's *The Gilded Age* goes West in search of a coal mine, and lives in the "faith" of discovering it, seeing himself as a "hermit" consecrated to a cause. "This is not mere zeal," observes Brooks, but "quite specifi-cally the zeal of the religious votary."[3] Perfectionism has another side too, the finicking, touch-me-not idealism which dares not wrestle with life as found. Hawthorne, who never evaded a responsibility, who paid every debt, had little use for the ingrown unanimity of a Brook Farm, when the world he knew was plainly and inevitably full of contradictions. He was willing to engage in life on its crude average level, to know and to deal with politics more intimately than any literary man of his day, and to accept as his best friends men who drew in the smoky air of contemporaneity with every breath. When he contemplated the perfectionist in Aylmer he saw, first of all, a symbol of exalted aesthetic aspiration. But he was undoubtedly aware of these ironic parallels also.

And for our second example: Hawthorne looked with stern suspicion upon the queen of Romantic faculties, that occult perspicacity which enables the artist to pierce the externals of his fellow creature, laying bare the heart's most intimate fears and desires. It is this knowledge of hidden weakness that may be supposed to enable the artist, like a modern psychologist, actually to predict the destiny of those he contemplates; such is the gift of the painter of "The Prophetic Pictures." But Hawthorne's prophetic painter is hardly a Carlylean figure. His preternatural vision is without power to illuminate others. Indeed, as will later be shown, he is not unrelated to some of Hawthorne's worst villains—to Roger Chillingworth, who explores with morbid passion the anguished heart of the man who has loved Hester, and whom Régis Michaud has compared to a psychiatrist who works a torture instead of a cure.[4] Indeed, there is a connection as well between those who intend no malice in their prying, like Hawthorne's artists Kenyon and Coverdale, and those who use their power for destruction —the mesmerists Westervelt and Matthew Maule, for example. *All* who possess this keenest perceptive power are deficient in feeling. For is the artist or scientist less selfishly exploitive than the mesmerist quack? Even to cultivate the power to discover human secrets out of detached curiosity is a sin—perhaps the source of that mysterious "unpardonable sin" which Ethan Brand sought and found in becoming "a cold observer looking on mankind as the subject of his experiment."[5] It is true that to some this insight comes unsought in Hawthorne's tales. But these, ironically, are men already guilty of some other sin—Dimmesdale, Roderick Elliston, and Young Goodman Brown—whose own corruption it is that enables them to see beneath the fine appearance others make—an ability, then, born of evil, and tainted by it.

What may be noted here, again, are some of the analogies that exist between this power and external social phenomena—analogies we are apt to lose sight of in the close psychological scale of Hawthorne's treatment. Stewart has acutely observed: "Hawthorne's mesmerists might be taken as types of a large class of men who impose their wills upon weaker wills and inexorably, as by a natural law, draw disciples and converts into their strong orbits: the political demagogue, the leader of reform, even the philosopher who warps lesser minds to his system."[6] Here too, then, as in the case of the perfectionist, it is possible that social parallels exist for Hawthorne's symbolic trait. An unprecedented public figure arose in Hawthorne's lifetime—the mass politician who, with consummate skill and few scruples, "delivered the vote" of the new urban populations. Westervelt, the grotesque Gothic humbug with the false teeth, is really not so unlike the Fernando Woods of the day, who gained their influence over others by a shrewd knowledge of the simple heart. And even the idealist Emerson, as Stewart points out, tended to become a doctrinaire apostle of his own light, mildly appropriating the wills of his followers by the charm and energy of his personality.[7] Surely some of these examples help to explain why Hawthorne suspected the Romantic faculty of insight, even in the artist.

Thus, in numerous ways, life itself must have acted as interpreter of the artist's destiny for Hawthorne. Upon the great screen of common experience the artist found his qualities magnified and distorted. His very virtues, such as his vaunted powers of perception, became the means whereby, in other spheres, social evil could be wrought, his idealist quest for ultimate perfection became suspect when expressed in terms of material objectives, and his self-absorption, a condition of his creativity, was rampant egotism when projected upon the scene of common life. Meanwhile, his personal experience enforced upon him the lesson that loneliness, the specific ordeal of so many creative Americans in Hawthorne's day and beyond, was somehow a natural destiny, an inevitable consequence of the artist's choice of role.

More obvious, perhaps, than society's own grotesque parody of the artist's gifts was the paradoxical fact that for the artist himself American life provided few meaningful outlets. The gifts of the mind, to which the expanding economy gave amplified scope in the play of industry or politics, were deprecated or made insignificant in the artist. In such a milieu, the genius of the organizer of manufacturing or of the financial wizard could reap a ripe reward; so also could the apposite mental energy of the inventor or the publicist. Yet when we speak, as we shall later have occasion to, of Hawthorne's lifelong inability to support his family on his literary earnings, it will be well to bear in mind that he died not the obscurest man of letters in America—as he had once called himself—but quite possibly the most eminent. It is striking how few of the great intellectuals of Hawthorne's time really solved the simple problem of earning a living. If they had no private incomes, they lived on the generosity of others, like Alcott, or accepted uncongenial and distracting jobs, as Hawthorne was forced to do. Indeed, Thoreau might have ended up a successful pencil manufacturer if he had not obstinately insisted on living on his own terms of minimal "practicality." The man who would, like Emerson, be defined by no other title than "scholar" was in reality professionless.

And more than mere bread and butter was missing from the board—not merely the fact that it was difficult to make letters pay gave the literary artist his sense of alienation. He felt that he lacked a "place," his true place, his sphere —like the bewildered caller in Hawthorne's "The Intelligence Office." The sense of a landscape and a tradition empty of those favoring presences that make for mature art —this was the mood that produced the first real American expatriates. Hiram Powers, whose "Greek Slave," in sugar-white alabaster copies, was widely admired, could argue that he simply earned more by working as a sculptor in Florence; there, the very atmosphere, dense with great art, drove up the price of commissions, the customer forgot the account books of his New England office, and superb marble and the most skilled craftsmen were available at bargain rates (X, 432). But Hawthorne understood that his friend Story and the rest of the American colony in Italy were held by a subtler appeal and he himself confessed in *Our Old Home* to a haunting "home-feeling" for the capital cities of historic culture, Rome and London.[8] More important, though, than the assets presented by a rich and ancient setting, more important than the well-known native paucity of ingredients, the absence of the "items of high civilization," as James would call them,[9] was probably the simple fact that life abroad externalized the spiritual expatriation, the iron severance from the common current, which the American intellectual now began to experience. Matthew Josephson has quoted on the title page of his *Portrait of the Artist as American*[10] a sentence of Melville's, "I feel I am an exile here." How true it is that the sense of exile *at home* was to be obscurely present in the consciousness of American artists throughout the second half of the nineteenth century. Melville and Hawthorne, like Emily Dickinson and Henry Adams, reacted to the quality of their experience not by foreign residence, but by an obsession with the theme of isolation.

Paul Elmer More was the first of many to observe that loneliness is the characteristic experience at the heart of all of Hawthorne's writing. He went on to say, however, as few have done, that Hawthorne was not expressing a purely personal but a universal predicament.[11] Rather too much has been made, as modern biographical research has made clear, of Hawthorne's personal reclusiveness, and of the significance of the "lonely chamber" period of his youth, which may not have been either so solitary or so melancholy as he himself romantically exaggerated it to be.[12] However biographical one chooses to make Hawthorne's legends of isolation, it is still true, in any case, that he was dramatizing the experience of many men. But the universality of the theme of loneliness should probably be identified more precisely than More thought necessary with the circumstances of life in Hawthorne's time, circumstances that affected the intellectual in particular. Loneliness was, to begin with, the characteristic experience of the American artist from Hawthorne's day onward, as we have just seen. And just as truly it must have been the fate of many others. There is no question that exceptional men have always experienced the isolating effects of those differences of achievement or ability that mark them off from the average; it does seem plain, however, that in the nineteenth century the conditions of life were creating a peculiar awareness of the difficulty of meeting one's fellow in trust and understanding. In a society that seemed only ready to pervert if it would not neglect the potencies of the gifted, isolation was a natural consequence for the man of brain who rejected the opportunities of the politician and the financier. We will shortly observe how Romanticism, the loose bundle of philosophic notions which nearly everyone—including Hawthorne—carried about with him in this period, characteristically includes a sense of the dislocation between the norm and the exception (although, of course, the exception is celebrated as the highest good); past ages had not concerned themselves so much with the *problem* of the peculiar or the gifted person. Romantic theory itself had, of course, a significant influence upon Hawthorne's views, as I shall shortly show, but equally significant, surely, is the fact that Hawthorne dwelt not only in an ambiance of ideas, but in a real world in which the theme of isolation had deep meaning. His interest in this theme was a reflection of experience as well as a phenomenon in the "history of ideas."

THE MATRIX OF THEORY

So far I have emphasized the way in which Hawthorne's approach to the artist is a part of his inspection of contemporary life, particularly of the role of the intellectual in that life. Plainly, however, it was also through ideas that Hawthorne confronted the problems presented by life— both the ideas that were on hand and the ideas, secured from an older heritage or worked out for himself, that he found to be more serviceable than the current stock. The contemporary matrix was transcendental. However often we shall have occasion to qualify the definition of Hawthorne as an Emersonian Romantic, there is no denying that he absorbed the elements of transcendentalism in common with his contemporaries and could no more have avoided the transcendental framework of ideas than he could have avoided acquiring the thousand touches of taste or accent that identified him as a New Englander of the nineteenth century. S. F. Gingerich observed some years ago that the transcendental principle "entered the world as a presence, a force, an atmosphere pervasive and inescapable even by those who by temperament and express purpose were least inclined to countenance it."[13] So it is that many of the materials of Hawthorne's mind and art are the common idealist furniture. Both from the Platonic strain in his Protestantism and from the current influence from Germany and England which swirled about his doorstep, Hawthorne imbibed easily recognized influences. His art is rooted in distinctions between the realms of the real and the ideal, and his taste for symbolism and allegory is obviously related to a metaphysics which saw the world as the manifestation of one essence. From his transcendentalism flowed the usual corollaries of Romantic ethics, psychology and aesthetics. He conceived of experience as having both an inner and an outer aspect, and of morals as resulting from the tension between "Head" and "Heart." He apparently accepted the distinctions between Understanding and Reason, Fancy and Imagination, the mechanical and the organic.

Yet while these antitheses are expressed in conventional Romantic terms, Hawthorne's handling of them often represents, as we shall observe, a criticism. The more one studies his work, the more evident it becomes that Hawthorne manipulates the Romantic machinery only to expose its hidden weaknesses. His most important judgments of life are anti-Romantic.

It must be admitted that much of this anti-Romanticism is as "romantic," in its way, as the cynicism of Byron or the pessimism of the *Sturm und Drang* writers in Germany. It is at least partly constructed out of the same copious storehouse as transcendentalism itself—but it is the negative, the dark, the Gothic side of Romanticism. Morse Peckham has suggested that the concept of a "negative Romanticism" would be useful in explaining certain aspects of the work of nearly all the English Romantics, and, taken as a whole, the work of Byron, who does not share the Romantic view of the imagination and otherwise fails to meet the standard qualifications for membership in the Romantic movement. This suggestion may be useful in our analysis of Hawthorne. Peckham defines negative Romanticism as the expression of the feelings and ideas of a man who has left the static mechanism of the eighteenth-century world behind, but has not yet arrived at the transcendentalist re-integration.[14] Such a state Peckham discerns as a temporary stage in *The Ancient Mariner, The Prelude,* and *Sartor Resartus,* an interlude of spiritual death which is succeeded by rebirth. Doubt, the sense of religious and social isolation, the separation of reason from creative power, mark this interval in the experience of Coleridge, Wordsworth, and Carlyle, and mark nearly the whole experience of Byron.

> The typical symbols of negative romanticism are individuals who are filled with guilt, despair, and cosmic and social alienation. They are often presented, for instance, as having committed some horrible and unmentionable crime in the past. They are often outcasts from men and God, and they are almost always wanderers over the face of the earth. They are Harolds, they are Manfreds, they are Cains. They are heroes of such poems as *Alastor.*[15]

And they are heroes of such stories as "Ethan Brand." When we speak of Hawthorne as a critic of Romanticism, it is well to bear in mind that it is positive Romanticism, specifically optimistic transcendentalism, that he ultimately criticizes. Unlike Carlyle, Hawthorne does not completely achieve an Everlasting Yea to succeed his Everlasting No. Melville observed, "He says No! in thunder; but the Devil himself cannot make him say *yes.*"[16] Actually, Hawthorne said Yes a good many times, though his strongest utterances, as I shall show, are negative.

But Hawthorne's attitude towards transcendentalism

sprang from deeper roots. As Melville also noticed, "this great power of blackness in him derives its force from its appeals to that Calvinistic sense of Innate Depravity and Original Sin, from whose visitations, in some shape or other, no deeply thinking mind is always and wholly free."[17] Where Hawthorne found that the Romantic viewpoint failed him, he made use of an older moral and philosophic tradition. From his Puritan inheritance—the conduit of his essential religiousness—he drew a moral seriousness which dissolved the Romantic veil. As Hyatt H. Waggoner has rightly emphasized,[18] Hawthorne's ethical or religious outlook has been too readily termed "Puritan," when in truth it is simply "Christian" in a sense already old at the Protestant Reformation. Historic Christianity—as exhibited in Saint Augustine, for example—is founded on the conviction of the reality and the opposition of good and evil and of man's propensity to sin, doctrines repellent to the Romantic optimism of Hawthorne's time. It is nevertheless true that in America this view had been emphatically expressed by the Puritans, that Puritanism provided native terms and symbols for it, and I feel that it is valid to continue to think of Hawthorne as having been aware of the "Puritan" tradition, the peculiarly native experience of Christian orthodoxy.

There has been a good deal of disagreement over Hawthorne's attitude toward his ancestors, springing, of course, from the obvious contradictions he took no trouble to conceal—the love and the hate, the sense of guilt in being different from them and the equal sense of guilt in being akin to them, the critical severity toward their superstitions and hardness of heart, and the readiness to utilize their quaint beliefs and harsh prejudices to paradoxically represent an unaltered validity. But it is clear, I think, that Henry James blundered seriously in his wonderfully urbane little study of Hawthorne when he declared that Hawthorne had converted the deepest principle of his inheritance "into one of his toys."

> Nothing is more curious and interesting than this almost exclusively *imported* character of the sense of sin in Hawthorne's mind; it seems to exist there merely for an artistic and literary purpose. He had ample cognizance of the Puritan conscience; it was his natural heritage; it was reproduced in him; looking into his soul, he found it there. But his relation to it was only, as one may say, intellectual; it was not moral and theological. He played with it, and used it as a pigment: he treated it, as the metaphysicians say, objectively. He was not discomposed, disturbed, haunted by it, in the manner of its usual and regular victims, who had not the little postern door of fancy to slip through, to the other side of the wall.[19]

Hawthorne truly had, he was disturbed by, the Puritan sense of sin—and in this he glared at his contemporaries across a gulf. Among his fellow-writers only Melville, as we have seen, stood on the same side of that gulf. Certainly his Concord neighbor, the great Emerson, was as Pelagian as Hawthorne was Augustinian. "I could never give much reality to evil and pain," he put down in his notebook on his fifty-eighth birthday, and though his strenuous optimism was more hardly earned than his more superficial admirers have always supposed, Emerson did ultimately reject the idea of original sin, whether as theologic doctrine or moral metaphor.[20] Melville admitted in *Billy Budd* that his Scriptural phrase, "the mystery of iniquity," was unlikely to commend his analysis of the dark character of Claggart to the contemporary reader, and that the doctrine of man's fall was "a doctrine now popularly ignored."[21] But Hawthorne, in his lifelong examination of the "foul cavern of the heart," to use one of his own iterative expressions, refuted the Romantic idea that man's nature is essentially good, even divine. Looking inward, this exemplary citizen and irreproachable family man was probably ready to acknowledge that there was no human foulness that was alien to him—*"homo sum. . . ."* Man must not disdain his brotherhood, even with the guiltiest, he declares in "Fancy's Show Box," "since, though his hand be clean, his heart has surely been polluted by the flitting phantoms of iniquity. He must feel that when he shall knock at the gate of heaven, no semblance of an unspotted life can entitle him to entrance there. Penitence must kneel, and Mercy come from the footstool of the throne, or that golden gate will never open!" (I, 257) This is the vantage point from which he judges the artist, that figure who represents the ultimate Romantic ideal of self-development, uniqueness, freedom, holiness—as a man among men.

The knowledge of good and evil represents for him the maturity of the human consciousness, as for the Lord and Lady of the May, in "The Maypole of Merrymount." If the Romantics were prone to wish themselves like unto little children, Hawthorne was readier to advise that a time comes to put away childish things. Dimmesdale's "Is not this better than what we dreamed of in the forest?" (V, 300) signifies this maturity. Rousseau had hailed the instinctive virtue of the savage and the child; Hawthorne's Donatello is a criticism of the "natural man" who must discover the sense of good and evil to be truly human; Pearl and the "brood of baby fiends" who assault the little Quaker Ilbrahim in "The Gentle Boy" illustrate the truth that good is not instinct within the human breast. We would naturally expect to find Hawthorne skeptical of the doctrine that the artist is like the child and the savage—a sort of wise fool in whom ordinary reason remains undeveloped, but who is inspired by the breath of the divine—*le souffle divin,* as Diderot called it.

In the traditional analysis of the fall of man lay, of course, a warning against both an unmeasured freedom of self-expression and an unconfined curiosity about nature's secrets. Yet these were the particular privileges accorded by Romantic theory to the artist, as well as to the scholar or scientific seeker with whom Hawthorne often identified him. Upstart pride, the foolish creature's presumption that it knows a better freedom than that of submission to the will of its Creator—this classic definition of the original fall must have seemed to Hawthorne to be still profoundly the error of fallen mankind. Pride is Hawthorne's master sin, as it is the deadliest of the seven for the Christian moralist. Lady Eleanore, whose gorgeous mantle brings a plague's infection, as her pride (of which it is a symbol) brings the vengeance of deformity and death, is only the most explicit of Hawthorne's many representations of the sin of pride. Pride is also the fatal failing of his seekers and scientists, his poets and artists. Particularly suspect to Hawthorne, therefore, was the Romantic artist's proud claim to freedoms transcending ordinary moral laws. And the desire for more knowledge than we need to attain heavenly bliss, the thirst, ever growing since the Renaissance, for more and more knowing of *all* things—this, too, could be viewed as a rehearsal of Adam and Eve's original inconsequence. Ethan Brand, Rappaccini, Aylmer are all clearly guilty of the lust for knowledge, but on a lower plane all those characters of Hawthorne's who are intemperately curious sin in the same primeval way. It is curiosity that repeatedly leads Hawthorne's artists into improper inquiry into hidden matters.

Hawthorne's acceptance of the myth of the fall, with all its ambiguous overtones of loss and gain, may be fundamentally connected with his analysis of the value of knowledge. If knowledge is the fruit of sin, it is, of course, purchased at the most terrible of prices. But such sin as purchases knowledge may, like the original fall, also be considered "fortunate," a condition of eventual growth into greater happiness. Between the two ancient views of the fall for which the Christian tradition gives sanction—that it was unqualified disaster for man and that it was a *"felix culpa"*—Hawthorne may not have seriously tried to choose. But the theological complexity may have served excellently to express his own mingled feelings concerning the value of knowledge. The famous argument in *The Marble Faun* should be seen as essentially unresolved. Sin and its attendant remorse had, Kenyon told the aseptic Hilda, developed in the faun "a thousand high capabilities, moral and intellectual, which we never should have dreamed of asking for, within the scanty compass of the Donatello whom we knew. . . . Is sin, then—which we deem such a dreadful blackness in the universe,—is it, like sorrow merely an element of human education through which we struggle to a higher and purer state than we could otherwise have attained? Did Adam fall that we might ultimately rise to a far loftier paradise than his?" But Hilda cries out, "Do not you perceive what a mockery your creed makes, not only of all religious sentiments, but of moral law?" (VI, 519-20) And so their problem remains poised between them.[22]

Of course, nothing better expresses Hawthorne's ambiguous balancing of the claims of innocence and experience, virtue and sin, ignorance and knowledge, than his disturbingly attractive portraits of his "dark ladies." Not only Miriam, Kenyon's preceptor in the view he expresses above, but Hester and Zenobia are illustrations of the intellectual power and personal magnetism which sin or some measure of participation in the dark side of experience has bestowed. Philip Rahv has argued in a notable essay that these heroines, who possess the attractiveness of vigorous life exceeding that of any others of Hawthorne's characters, are also condemned most severely because of the author's mingled longing for and fear of the life of the physical senses.[23] Just as ambiguous, I would add, is Hawthorne's appraisal of knowledge, the fruit of experience and, in the theological sense, of sin. It, too, is profoundly alluring and profoundly menacing, like these heroines who have won an intenser being from the taste of forbidden fruit. And yet, by union with this siren is the artist made. He may save his soul only by renouncing her—and renouncing his art—by loving instead white innocence, symbolized by those blond, unfallen virgins, Priscilla, Phoebe, and Hilda. Union with these represents a return to Eden, to pastoral simplicity, a surrender of knowledge and art. Sometimes, however, the commitment to experience has gone too far. There is no redemptive return—and no blond sweetheart—for Arthur Dimmesdale or for Giovanni Guasconti, the young scholar who drinks too deep of knowledge in "Rappaccini's Daughter."

Beatrice Rappaccini is the first of Hawthorne's dark heroines, and her story is his most powerful statement of the ambiguity of knowledge. Beautiful and baleful, glowing with powerful life and conveying death in her touch, she seems to symbolize that augmented vitality won, at the price of death, from the experience of evil. That Hawthorne had the myth of the fall of man in mind when he wrote "Rappaccini's Daughter," is made very clear. Beatrice has been nourished by a man-created tree of knowledge, the poisonous plant which is described as the offspring of her father's science (II, 142). Both plant and Beatrice have matured in a mysterious garden which Giovanni first glimpses from the secret vantage point of his window. As the young man observes the strange, cautious bearing of the old gardener he is, in fact, reminded of the first of gardens. "It was strangely frightful to the young man's imagination to see this air of insecurity in a person cultivating a garden, that most simple and innocent of human toils, and which had been alike the joy and labor of the unfallen parents of the race. Was this garden, then, the Eden of the present world? And this man, with such a perception of harm in what his own hands caused to grow,—was he the Adam?" (II, 112)

We learn that Dr. Rappaccini cultivates his strange herbs according to an ancient theory—"that all medicinal virtues are comprised within those substances we term vegetable poisons" (II, 117). This is an apt representation of the mixed nature of knowledge, it may be noted. Hawthorne, approaching the subject from the older, Christian standpoint, felt that man may have a perverse relation to Nature when he seeks her secrets, like Rappaccini, with "a look as deep as Nature itself, but without Nature's warmth of love" (II, 125). The beautiful and poisonous Beatrice, like the plants in her father's garden, is the result of an "adultery" of intentions, a tragic mixture of innocence and corruption. "The production was no longer of God's making, but the monstrous offspring of man's depraved fancy, glowing with only an evil mockery of beauty" (II, 128). Just such a mixture also is the feeling Beatrice inspires in Giovanni, "a wild offspring of both love and horror that had each parent in it (II, 123). As the doomed girl and her lover stand before him, Rappaccini is seen to gaze upon them. His attitude presents us with a final symbolic representation of ambiguous power. He spreads his hands above them, says Hawthorne, "in the attitude of a father imploring a blessing upon his children; but those were the same hands that had thrown poison into the stream of their lives" (II, 146).

There is a link between Rappaccini and the "scholar-idealists" of Hawthorne's tales, however different from theirs his character appears. For Rappaccini also has lofty motives. Is he not "a noble spirit," asks young Giovanni (who is himself a student), for "are there many men capable of so spiritual a love of science?" (II, 117) He is, indeed, a later Adam, tempted to his fall by the noblest of temptations, the desire for more knowledge than the human lot

requires. In the scene of ambiguous benediction just referred to, he gazes upon the youth and maiden who are his
work "as might an artist who should spend his life in achieving a picture or a group of statuary and finally be satisfied
with his success." That the comparison is more than accidental we shall see when we come to examine Hawthorne's artist-figures.

Hawthorne seems ready to assert, at times, the converse
of Christ's words, "If ye were blind, ye should have no sin."
As he shows us the effects of sin in many characters, he seems
to imply that only if ye sin, ye have sight—the absence of
sin is blindness. It is as a consequence of sin that one gains
above all the power to *see* into the mysteries of others. After
his own experience of evil-doing the Reverend Mr. Dimmesdale acquires that knowledge of the human heart which
enables him to preach with a profundity never before heard
from him; after his participation in the Devil's sacrament
Young Goodman Brown sees the hidden damnation in his
fellow villagers, and Roderick Elliston's "bosom serpent"
enables him to perceive the reptile of evil coiled within the
breast of each man he meets. However Hawthorne resolves
the theological paradox of the fortunate fall, there is no
doubt that in his fiction the sense of guilt is always attached
to the fruits of knowledge, particularly to the ability to see
where others are blind—the artist's special gift of vision as
the Romantics celebrated it.

But one may characterize Hawthorne's attitude not only
as Christian but as classical. In some of his favorite eighteenth-century writers, whose graceful and "social" style his
own reflects, he found further correctives to Romanticism.
The eighteenth century's assumption that the real world
of objects was indeed "real" must have abetted his anti-
transcendentalism. In England he visited Johnson's birthplace at Lichfield and later reflected that a "gross diet" of
that robust, objective writer was "wholesome food" for one

whose "native propensities were towards Fairy Land" (VII, 150-51). Moreover, in his fiction Hawthorne placed man, the social animal, at the center of his universe, as had the ancients, the philosophers of the Renaissance, and the Englishmen of Johnson's time. Like them, he was interested in the classic problem of man and the community—he was, as Stewart says, "an analyst of human relations, of the nice relationship of person to person, of the adjustment of the individual to society,"[24] A chief theme, for example, of *The Scarlet Letter* is the tragedy of segregation. The superiority of Hester's penance over Dimmesdale's does not consist in its intensity—indeed the minister is plainly the greater sufferer of the two and perhaps most aware of the theological significance of their sin. But Hester's public shame, her very ostracism, establishes for her a sounder connection with the social whole than does Dimmesdale's secret self-chastisement. The tragedy of their crime is that it is like the character of Pearl which "lacked reference and adaptation to the world into which she was born" (V, 114).

Yes, Hawthorne was concerned with the collective as well as the individual, and it is for this reason that his work presents a seeming paradox: he peoples his fiction with examples of human character of an eccentricity almost past belief—in what world of the probable would we expect to meet Wakefield, the Reverend Mr. Hooper, Lady Eleanore? —but he labors to achieve the disclosure of universal nature, the norm. His method is symbolic or allegorical rather than realistic, certainly, but his intention is classical. He aimed his researches, as he declared, "into the depths of our common nature" (III, 386). Such an effort is classically humanistic, for it conceives of a centrality in human nature, a universal which it is man's function to fulfill, rather than to flout by the devices of egotism.

Thus, Hawthorne did not romanticize loneliness or the separate personal expansion of the ego, but condemned them. His criticism of the introspective, what we would call the seclusive, nature, in Roger Elliston, Hepzibah Pyncheon, Parson Hooper, Reuben Bourne, Arthur Dimmesdale, and others, is not unconnected with his suspicion of the intellectual who sets himself to lonely self-contemplation, becoming fatally aloof from humanity unless love seals the rift, as it does for Elliston and Hepzibah. Hawthorne's own life, as we shall see, was itself a struggle to escape the bonds of seclusion. Like his artists Kenyon and Drowne, he discovered that the love even of one other being was a transforming influence. His art itself was designed from the very start "to open an intercourse with the world" (I, 17).

To the Romantics, egotism was divine. But in his fiction Hawthorne shows us repeatedly that he felt no achievement of personal development to be worth the price of exclusion from the hand-in-hand of common brotherhood. Hester Prynne's Romantic self-realization stirs Hawthorne's sympathies but not his ultimate sanction, and makes her an isolated and tragic figure. It is the particular tragedy of all his exceptional persons—his scholars, reformers, scientists, artists—that, like Ethan Brand, who cultivated his powers "to the highest point of which they were susceptible" (III, 494), or Richard Digby, whose narrow plank of creed was fashioned for his own salvation only, they discover that in perfecting their gifts they have turned their hearts to stone.

Hence, though Hawthorne's writing expresses the heightened Romantic interest in subjectivity or the inner consciousness,[25] the Romantic emphasis on what the Germans call *Bildung* did not appeal to him. To develop one's own faculties at all costs did not appear to him to be godlike, but simply *inhuman*. To give free reign to one's peculiarities, like a Byronic hero, or declare with Emerson that "nothing is at last sacred but the integrity of your own mind,"[26] must have seemed to him a degrading of man's true end. While Emerson, as James put it, was helping Americans "to take a picturesque view of one's internal possibilities and to find in the landscape of the soul all sorts of fine sunrise and moonlight effects,"[27] Hawthorne's inward glance disclosed the sterner prospect of human nature limited, fallible, wayward. His wife Sophia Peabody's transcendental enthusiasms notwithstanding, he found the transcendentalists he encountered to be full of a dangerous self-absorption. He complained that Emerson's disciples were "imbued with a false originality," adding: "This triteness of novelty is enough to make any man of common sense blaspheme at all ideas of less than a century's standing, and pray that the world may be petrified and rendered immovable in precisely the worst moral and physical state that it ever yet arrived at, rather than be benefited by such schemes of such philosophers" (II, 43). Ellery Channing, for example, was one of those "originals in a small way" who "after one has seen a few of them, become more dull and common-place than even those who keep the ordinary pathway of life."[28] And Margaret Fuller was "a great humbug" who had "stuck herself full of borrowed qualities which she chose to provide herself with, but which had no root in her."[29] One suspects that Hawthorne's hostility to such a program was somehow involved in his monumental boredom with the self-cultivation so tirelessly practiced by Sophia during their European travels. Though he made some attempt to develop his untrained taste, he was driven to confess himself a victim to "that icy demon of weariness, who haunts great picture galleries." I imagine this was partly because he felt (in the age which initiated mass education) that the effort at self-refinement was really not worthwhile. In defining Margaret's character, Hawthorne expressed his conviction that human nature was essentially intractable, even predetermined by forces beyond our conscious control:

She took credit to herself for having been her own Redeemer, if not her own Creator; and indeed, she was far more a work of art than any of Mozier's statues. But she was not working on inanimate substance, like marble or clay; there was something within her that she could not possibly come at, to re-create it and refine it; and, by and by, this rude old potency bestirred itself, and undid all her labor in the twinkling of an eye.[30]

And there is more than humor in his suggestion that Margaret had forgotten who made her. One can recall—as Hawthorne may have—how Milton's Satan urged his followers to doubt that God had ever created them.[31] He may have heard from Sophia of those meetings of transcendental ladies which Miss Fuller conducted, and of one occasion when she was reported to have declared:

Love and creativeness are dynamic forces, out of which we, individually, as creatures, go forth bearing his [God's] image; that is, having within our being the same dynamic forces by which we also add constantly to the total sum of existence, and shaking off ignorance, and its effects, and by becoming more ourselves, *i.e.,* more divine—destroying sin in its principle, we attain to absolute freedom, we return to God, conscious like himself, and, as his friends, giving, as well as receiving, felicity forevermore.[32]

Nature, as he wrote in "The Birthmark," "permits us, indeed, to mar, but seldom to mend, and, like a jealous patentee, on no account to make" (II, 54).

He did not believe that man was "free," as the Romantics liked to suppose. Man, to him, was not an inexhaustible reservoir of possibilities. Emerson declared: "I shun father and mother and wife and brother, when my genius calls me. I would write on the lintels of the door-post, *Whim.*"[33] But Hawthorne's "Wakefield" is a parable of the fatal effects of free will unthinkingly invoked. A child's ramble is soon over, but a man may find, like the narrator in "Little Annie's Rambles," that he has "gone too far astray for the town crier to call [him] back" (I, 152). It sometimes must have seemed to Hawthorne that the artist was in danger of becoming a sort of Wakefield of the imagination whose one initial step outside the common experience proves fatal. Ever after he is doomed to look upon other men, even upon his closest and most loved ones, from an unseen vantage point, only a handbreadth away, yet remote as another world.

Life, far from being subject to the will, was full of obscurity and compulsion. Wakefield's story illustrated to Hawthorne "how an influence beyond our control lays its strong hand on every deed which we do and weaves its consequences into the iron tissue of necessity" (I, 160). Another story, "David Swan," has as its theme the thought that "we can be but partially acquainted even with the events which actually influence our course through life, and our final destiny. There are innumerable other events—if such they may be called—which come close upon us, yet pass away without actual results, or even betraying their near approach by the reflection of any light or shadow across our minds" (I, 211). In *The Marble Faun*, again, Hawthorne remarks that "the actual experience of even the most ordinary life is full of events that never explain themselves, either as regards their origin or their tendency" (VI, 514).

We are now in a position to understand how coldly Hawthorne would view the exaltation of the powers of mind which is central to Romanticism. As we have seen, there was much in the world he contemplated to promote his sensitive recoil from the application of those powers. While many of the thinkers and poets of his time hailed the prospect of social and material progress achieved by the new partnership of men with Nature, Hawthorne appears to anticipate

the view of later generations, which were to find that none
of the old human evils of social or personal life had passed
away with the increase of man's knowledge. In Hawthorne's
portraits of intellectuals we see repeated demonstration of
his warning that the isolated life and aim, the exaltation of
the will, the monomaniac subordination of personal feelings to impersonal goals, can yield only evil.

NOTES TO CHAPTER I

[1] *Nathaniel Hawthorne: A Biography* (New Haven: Yale University
Press, 1948), p. 253. Earlier critics—W. C. Brownell, Lloyd Morris,
V. L. Parrington, V. F. Calverton, and Granville Hicks—charged
Hawthorne with ignorance of and indifference to contemporary social
issues, and believed that these attitudes fatally weakened his art.
In a well-known passage in his *Main Currents in American Thought*
(New York: Harcourt, Brace and Co., 1927, 1930), Parrington called
Hawthorne "the extreme and finest expression of the refined aliena-
tion from reality that in the end palsied the creative mind of New
England" (II, 450). Other scholars—especially Stewart—have, however, so strengthened our view of a Hawthorne who knew and cared
about the problems of his time that there is today little accord with
the idea that Hawthorne's mind was stimulated only by abstract moral
problems—or by the past.

[2] *The Age of Jackson* (Boston: Little, Brown and Co., 1945), p. 507.

[3] *The Ordeal of Mark Twain* (New York: E. P. Dutton and Co.,
1920), pp. 78-80.

[4] "Le traitment que Chillingworth fait subir à sa victime entend
bien être une torture et non une cure..." (*Le Roman americain
d'aujourd'hui; critique d'une civilization* [Paris: Boivin et Cie., 1926],
p. 29).

[5] *The Complete Works of Nathaniel Hawthorne, with Introductory
Notes,* ed. George Parsons Lathrop (Riverside ed.; Boston and New
York: Houghton, Mifflin and Co., 1883), III, 495. All subsequent page
and volume references to Hawthorne's writings will be to this edition.

[6] Stewart, *Nathaniel Hawthorne,* p. 251.

7 *Idem.*

8 "... as long as either of those two great cities shall exist, the cities of the Past and of the Present, a man's native soil may crumble beneath his feet without leaving him altogether homeless upon earth" (VII, 256).

9 James' well-known enumeration of these items runs: "No State, in the European sense of the word, and indeed barely a specific national name. No sovereign, no court, no personal loyalty, no aristocracy, no church, no clergy, no army, no diplomatic service, no country gentlemen, no palaces, no castles, nor manors, nor old country-houses, nor parsonages, nor thatched cottages, nor ivied ruins; no cathedrals, nor abbeys, nor little Norman churches; no great Universities nor public schools—no Oxford, nor Eton, nor Harrow; no literature, no novels, no museums, no pictures, no political society, no sporting class —no Epsom nor Ascot!" *Hawthorne* (English Men of Letters Series; New York: Harper & Bros., 1879), pp. 42-43.

10 New York: Harcourt, Brace and Co., 1930.

11 "The Solitude of Nathaniel Hawthorne," *Shelburne Essays, First Series* (New York: G. P. Putnam's Sons, 1904), pp. 22-51.

12 Cf. Stewart, *Nathaniel Hawthorne*, pp. 35-44.

13 *Essays in the Romantic Poets* (New York: The Macmillan Co., 1924), p. 11.

14 "Towards a Theory of Romanticism," *PMLA*, LXVI (1951), 3-32.

15 *Ibid.*, p. 20.

16 Letter to Hawthorne, March, 1851, in *Herman Melville: Representative Selections*, ed. Willard Thorp (New York: American Book Company, 1938), p. 388.

17 "Hawthorne and his Mosses," *The Literary World*, August 17 and 24, 1850, reprinted in *ibid.*, p. 333.

18 *Hawthorne: A Critical Study* (Cambridge, Mass.: Harvard University Press, 1955), p. 14.

19 James, *Hawthorne*, p. 57.

20 As the editors of the new edition of the *Journals* point out, the genteel, idealistic, optimistic Emerson of the *Essays* suppressed the Emerson who occasionally revealed other sides of himself in his private writing. This second Emerson was in turn almost edited out of the *Journals* when they were published. Of some of the excluded passages, now finally printed, the editors write: "If the concern with sin is not obsessive here or elsewhere, the young Emerson's intense conviction of sin still suggests more kinship between him and Nathaniel Hawthorne than we have hitherto realized." *The Journals and Miscellane-*

ous Notebooks of Ralph Waldo Emerson, ed. William H. Gilman *et al.* (Cambridge, Mass.: Harvard University Press, 1960) , I, xxvii.

[21] *Billy Budd,* ed. F. Barron Freeman (Cambridge, Mass.: Harvard University Press, 1948) , pp. 147, 189.

[22] Critics have debated the final position of Hawthorne on this question. Interpretations vary between that of Austin Warren, who believes that Hilda expresses Hawthorne's last word, his conviction that sin "is not educative but warping" (*Hawthorne: Representative Selections,* pp. xxix-xxxi) , and Randall Stewart's conclusion that Kenyon's thesis "would seem to be the author's whole theme" (*Nathaniel Hawthorne,* p. 264) .

[23] "The Dark Lady of Salem," in *Image and Idea* (A New Directions Paperback; New York: New Directions, 1957) .

[24] Stewart, *Nathaniel Hawthorne,* p. 252.

[25] Yet Hawthorne has been categorized as "Romantic" on this basis alone. Paul Kaufman (in *The Reinterpretation of American Literature,* ed. Norman Foerster [New York: Harcourt, Brace and Co., 1928], p. 125) calls Hawthorne and Melville "romancers par excellence," the former having "created an original introvert form true to his character, thus introducing the recent romantic preoccupation with individual feeling and imagination into the traditional type."

[26] "Self-Reliance," *The Complete Works of Ralph Waldo Emerson,* ed. Edward W. Emerson (Centenary ed.; Boston and New York: Houghton, Mifflin and Co., 1903-1904) , II, 50.

[27] James, *Hawthorne,* p. 83.

[28] *The American Notebooks by Nathaniel Hawthorne,* ed. Randall Stewart (New Haven: Yale University Press, 1932) , p. 168. All references to the *American Notebooks* will be to this edition, except for those passages missing from the Morgan manuscript and reproduced only in Mrs. Hawthorne's edition, included in the *Complete Works.*

[29] "It was such an awful joke that she should have resolved—in all sincerity, no doubt—to make herself the greatest, wisest, best woman of the age; and, to that end, she set to work on her strange, heavy, unpliable, and in many respects defective and evil nature, and adorned it with a mosaic of admirable qualities, such as she chose to possess; putting in here a splendid talent, and there a moral excellence, and polishing each separate piece, and the whole together, till it seemed to shine afar and dazzle all who saw it" (*The French and Italian Notebooks,* April 3, 1858) . Mrs. Hawthorne omitted Hawthorne's comments on Margaret Fuller in her edition of the *Notebooks* (Vol. X of the "Riverside" *Works*) , but they were printed by Julian Hawthorne

in *Nathaniel Hawthorne and His Wife* (Boston: James R. Osgood and Co., 1884) , I, 259-62.

30 *Hawthorne and His Wife,* I, 261.

31 *Paradise Lost,* V, 853-63.

32 Quoted in *The American Transcendentalists,* ed. Perry Miller (Doubleday Anchor Books; New York: Doubleday and Co., 1957) , p. 103.

33 "Self-Reliance," *Works,* II, 51.

Chapter II

Hawthorne's Romantic Aesthetics

~~~~~~

When one recognizes how Hawthorne set himself athwart much of Romanticism, particularly its optimistic ethics—its cheerful view of the nature of men and of their relations with one another—it is astounding to realize how large a Romantic residue remains in his thinking. I am particularly concerned here, of course, with his approach to art and artists, and it is precisely in this area of his thought that the conflict of Romantic and anti-Romantic tendencies is most critical. For art is the keystone of the Romantic arch; the artist himself is Romanticism's most defining symbol. Hawthorne could not help absorbing, I shall show, much of the aesthetic vapor that then so heavily charged the intellectual atmosphere, that surrounded the humblest scribbler or dauber, and from which the arts are still not completely free. And yet he saw the artist and his work from the remoter vantage point of the criticisms sketched in the previous chapter. Working from within the scented heart of Romantic idealism, he was yet capable of detecting sinister possibilities unperceived by most of his generation, and for the rapturous positives of idealist aesthetics he substituted a sterner judgment which placed a negative sign against Romanticism's most cherished hero—the artist.

I shall look first at the elements in Hawthorne's view of the artistic function which must be frankly labeled "transcendental" before examining the presence in his fiction of a major criticism of these same elements. In the section that follows I shall present what seems to me a substantial case for the idea that Hawthorne's view of the artist was a conventional Romantic one. From numerous scattered expressions in his notebooks and letters, and even in the fiction, one gets the impression that, like the Peabodys and their transcendental friends, he accepted the Romantic gospel of art, that gospel which in the thirties and forties entered so thrillingly into the New England consciousness, through Wordsworth and Coleridge and through the new philosophy of German idealism opened to view by Victor Cousin and Carlyle.

I must confess that this evidence, as it began to accumulate during early stages of this inquiry, at first disturbed me —for the grand design of Hawthorne's imaginative art already appeared to express a contrary viewpoint, manifested less explicitly, but more profoundly. Here there seemed to arise an instance when conscious opinion, the actual "I think . . ." of an author, might have to be put aside in favor of opinion drawn by inference from his creative exercises. I shall present, to begin with, the picture that very easily composes itself from many of Hawthorne's dispersed remarks on art. But I shall follow this thesis with its antithesis: Hawthorne's view of the artist as it emerges in the integrated patterns of his creative work, with, I feel, a quite indisputable definiteness of another sort. The contradiction, though it complicates, should not render our search fruitless. Isolable, quotable "opinion," which shall mainly occupy us now, may seem to demonstrate that Hawthorne was thoroughly an idealist who conceived of the artist in terms of current jargon. But the *configurations* of Hawthorne's legends, their tensions of narrative and character, symbol and tone, tell a contrary story. It is highly significant, it seems to me, that Hawthorne's judgments on the fine arts furnish some of our best evidence of his conscious idealism. They are a disclosure—one is tempted to say an exposure—of opinions which expressed themselves where his sensibility was *least* active.

It is undeniable that Hawthorne gave conscious assent to the transcendental view of art: a presentation of that ideal of which the visible world is but an imperfect expression. Nearly all nineteenth-century speculation acknowledged in some fashion the Platonic doctrine of ideas, certainly one of the most enduring philosophic notions of the West. But while Plato had deprecated the work of art as a "copy of a copy" of the reality residing in the realm of pure noumena, transcendental philosophy adopted the more flattering neo-Platonic view that the artist refashions Nature into art in the same way that God creates, achieving an ideality even superior to Nature's.

The Platonic strain is felt throughout Hawthorne's writing. Perhaps it goes far to explain his persistent allegorizing in the stories and novels. The fact is clear, at any rate, that the relationship between appearance and reality was always a dramatic problem to him, both as man and writer. To begin with, of course, Hawthorne accepted the proposition that reality is a spiritual rather than a material fact. Throughout the strange two years—1839 and 1840— during which he worked as a measurer of coal and salt in the Boston Custom House, he seems to have been particularly conscious of the divided nature of existence—perhaps because his own thoughts were so fantastically divided between the materiality of his duties and the creative exercises which they obstructed, perhaps even because of his disembodied love-life, a thing chiefly of dreams and of letters by which he was compelled to express to his absent (as well as transcendental) beloved the untenuous passion of a man of thirty-five. He wrote to Sophia of the two journals he thought of keeping, that of the inner and that of the outer life. "What a dry, dull history" the diary of external life would be, he exclaimed. "But then, apart from this, I would write another journal, of my inward life throughout the selfsame day. . . . Nobody would think that the same man could live two such different lives simultaneously. But then . . . the grosser life is a dream, and the spiritual life is a reality."[1] In the most famous of the extraordinary letters he wrote to Sophia at this time, he does, it is true, declare that love will rescue him from the kingdom of shadows ("We are not endowed with real life, and all that seems most real about us is but the thinnest substance of a dream—till the heart is touched"), but it is well to note that the therapeutic reality he speaks of is the eternal realm of pure spirit ("Then we begin to be—thereby we are beings of reality and inheritors of eternity").[2] One must observe at this point that Hawthorne's appetite for external life was even at this period much stronger than these quotations convey; like subsequent stages in his career, this one exhibits his life-long attempt to participate in and understand the realistic surface of his times. But the idealist concept of the pre-eminence of spirit over matter was nevertheless an inextricable part of his thinking.

So, on the Boston wharves, literally measuring the ponderable as a weigher of coal and salt, he was aware of what Blake called the "invisible universe" which is blocked from our sight by the material mirage of Urizen. Admittedly, he had, as Stuart Sherman observed, "a certain disdain for primary meanings, for the immediate gross reports of the senses. His imagination he sets continually at work contriving an avenue of escape from the vulgar and the humdrum."[3] On a day in February he notes with transcendental flute-notes the effort of the poor wingless biped man to raise himself a little above the earth:

How much mud and mire, how many pools of unclean water, how many slippery foot-steps, and perchance heavy tumbles, might be avoided, if one could tread but six inches above the crust of this world. Physically we cannot do this; our bodies cannot; but it seems to me that our hearts and minds may keep themselves above moral mud-puddles and other discomforts of the soul's pathway (IX, 214).[4]

As he tallies the loads of two sets of coal-shovelers in the bleak, wet air on the docks, he declares with a certain desperation:

> I was conscious that all this was merely a vision and a fantasy, and that, in reality, I was not half frozen by the bitter blast nor tormented by those grimy coal-heavers, but that I was basking quietly in the sunshine of eternity. . . . Any sort of bodily and earthly torment may serve to make us sensible that we have a soul that is not within the jurisdiction of such shadowy demons—it separates the immortal within us from the mortal. But the wind has blown my brains into such confusion that I cannot philosophize now (IX, 217).

Though more of such remarks seem to emanate from Hawthorne's period of courtship than from any other time, he was never to surrender the idealist point of view completely. At Brook Farm, though he manfully did his share of labor, he declared: "The real Me was never an associate of the community; there has been a spectral appearance there, sounding the horn at daybreak and milking the cows, and hoeing potatoes, and raking hay, toiling in the sun and doing me the honor to assume my name, but this spectre was not myself" (IX, 237).

Years later, in England, it was a hearty dinner of mutton chops and gooseberry pudding that was the chief consummation ("after coming so far to indulge a solemn and high emotion") of his visit to Dr. Johnson's Uttoxeter. As he

looked back upon the experience in *Our Old Home,* he
decided that, after all,

> A sensible man had better not let himself be betrayed into
> these attempts to realize the things which he has dreamed
> about, and which, when they cease to be purely ideal in his
> mind, will have lost the truest of their truth, the loftiest and
> profoundest part of their power over his sympathies. Facts
> as we really find them, whatever poetry they may involve, are
> covered with a stony excrescence of prose, resembling the
> crust on a beautiful sea-shell, and they never show their most
> delicate and divinest colors until we shall have dissolved
> away their grosser actualities by steeping them long in a
> powerful menstruum of thought. And seeking to actualize
> them again, we do but renew the crust. If this were otherwise,
> —if the moral sublimity of a great fact depended in any
> degree on its garb of external circumstances, things which
> change and decay,—it could not itself be immortal and ubiq-
> uitous, and only a brief point of time and a little neighbor-
> hood would be spiritually nourished by its grandeur and
> beauty (VII, 165-66).

He had come too close to the "crust" of actuality, and would
have done better to have imagined Dr. Johnson's famous
place of penance from afar—"for I found it holy to my con-
templation, again, as soon as it lay behind me." And he
reflected: "It but confirms what I have been saying, that
sublime and beautiful facts are best understood when
etherealized by distance" (VII, 168).

Only the "powerful menstruum of thought," the *acqua
regia* of the artistic imagination, can dissolve away the crust
that covers the Platonic "fact." The artist, of course, plays
a peculiarly exalted part in Romantic theory precisely because it is he alone who passes between the real and the
illusional, creating, after God's own fashion, a representation of the spirit immanent in all Nature. If everything, as
Sybil Dacy says in *Septimius Felton,* "has its spiritual mean-

ing which to the literal meaning is what the soul is to the body," then what is the artist's task? In *The House of the Seven Gables*, Hawthorne defined the poetic instinct as "the gift of discerning in this sphere of strangely mingled elements the beauty and the majesty which are compelled to assume a garb so sordid" (III, 59). Among the aesthetic company described in *The Marble Faun*, he describes a landscape painter whose love of and intimacy with Nature enabled him to reproduce her so that his pictures seemed "the reality of a better earth" (VI, 160). Literal realism was, in fact, the enemy of the artist's truer vision. When Hawthorne viewed the statues in Westminster Abbey he explained the inaccurate portraiture of many of the pieces as follows: "In truth, the artist (unless there be a divine efficacy in his touch, making evident a heretofore hidden dignity in the actual form) feels it an imperious law to remove his subject as far from the aspect of ordinary life as may be possible without sacrificing every trace of resemblance" (VII, 310).

Such an approach to reality and to art produces certain familiar corollaries, which one is not surprised to find present in Hawthorne's thinking. The idealist concept of art leads to a contempt for the materials of art since they *are* material, and to an emphasis on subject rather than on technique, on the artist's vision and intention rather than on the exact appearance of the embodied idea. The actual work on Greek vases and statues was done by slaves, we are told, and the practice of the sculptors Hawthorne knew expressed the same idealist contempt for the actual art-work compared with the artist's original "vision." Hawthorne found it vaguely "not quite pleasant" that these sculptors delegated the execution of their masterpieces to some "merely mechanical" person (X, 72). Yet, though his craftsman's respect for craft made him pause in doubt before a piece of sculpture which the "sculptor's" hand had never touched, he gave considerable assent to the theory which sustained it.

His own comments on art reveal that he was interested chiefly in the character of the artist's inspiration rather than in the technical qualities of the art-work. A definite theory of art explains the reactions which seem at first to be merely the result of Hawthorne's ignorance. He praised Guido, Fra Angelico, Sodoma, and Perugino, for example, for the qualities of inspiration he found in their work. Guido's "Michael" was "surely one of the most beautiful things in the world, one of the human conceptions that are imbued most deeply with the celestial" (X, 96). He thought the "Madonna della Seggiola" of Raphael the most beautiful picture in the world, with sanctity in its aspect, since this was an early work "when he mixed more religion with his paint than afterwards" (X, 370, 374). Perugino, he wrote, "is the first painter whose works seem really worth preserving for the genuine merit that is in them, apart from any quaintness and curiosity of an ancient and new-born art. Probably his religion was more genuine than Raphael's and therefore the Virgin often revealed herself to him in a loftier and sweeter face of divine womanhood than all the genius of Raphael could produce" (X, 320). Fra Angelico, also, "produces such a Christ, and such a Virgin, and such Saints, as he could not have foreseen, except in pure and holy imagination, nor have wrought out without saying a prayer between every two touches of his brush" (X, 320). He condemned the British painters whose work he saw at the Manchester Arts Exhibition because "they cannot paint anything high, heroic, and ideal"[5] but he felt that the canvasses of Hunt and a few other Pre-Raphaelites "were the only modern pictures that accomplish a higher end than that of pleasing the eye—the only ones that really take hold of the mind."[6] Hilda's disillusion with the qualities of her favorite old masters (in the chapter of *The Marble Faun*

titled "The Emptiness of Picture Galleries") brings her the
realization that too many of the artists had worked only to
satisfy the eye, without drawing upon the fountain of the
soul.

> She began to suspect that some, at least, of her venerated
> painters, had left an inevitable hollowness in their works,
> because, in the most renowned of them, they essayed to ex-
> press to the world what they had not in their own souls. They
> deified their light and wandering affections, and were con-
> tinually playing off the tremendous jest, alluded to above, of
> offering the features of some venal beauty to be enshrined in
> the holiest places. A deficiency of earnestness and absolute
> truth is generally discoverable in Italian pictures after the
> art had become consummate. When you demand what is
> deepest, these painters have not wherewithal to respond.
> They substituted a keen intellectual perception and a marvel-
> lous knack of external arrangement, instead of the live sym-
> pathy and sentiment which should have been their inspira-
> tion (VI, 386).

It is only fair to point out that such description of the effect
of art is not necessarily the result of a parochial taste—
though Hawthorne's actual interest in and knowledge of
painting was limited. The artists whom Hawthorne knew
would probably have written no differently, and their work
itself (now mostly hidden in the storage rooms of American
museums) bears out the truth that they also conceived of
their activities as Hawthorne did. Van Wyck Brooks has
observed that the Yankee sculptors and painters whom
Hawthorne met in Italy were preoccupied with storytelling. They turned out Greek slaves and Libyan sibyls,
Zenobia out of the novel by William Ware, allegories representing the struggles of genius, and so on.[7] Such an art of
embodied sentiment appealed to Hawthorne, who ap-
proached it as we would expect, not by examining externals, but by apprehending the "idea."

The work of art itself was viewed as inferior to this immaterial idea. In "The Artist of the Beautiful," Hawthorne writes:

> Alas that the artist, whether in poetry, or whatever other material, may not content himself with the inward enjoyment of the beautiful, but must chase the flitting mystery beyond the verge of his ethereal domain, and crush its frail being in seizing it with a material grasp. Owen Warland felt the impulse to give external reality to his ideas as irresistibly as any of the poets or painters who have arrayed the world in a dimmer and fainter beauty, imperfectly copied from the richness of their vision (II, 516).

Here Hawthorne expresses the final Romantic renunciation of the work of art in favor of the vision of the ideal which it crudely represents. Emerson declared in "Art" that "the arts, as we know them, are but initial. Our best praise is given to what they aimed and promised, not to the actual result. . . . There is a higher work for Art than the arts. They are abortive births, of an imperfect or vitiated instinct. Art is the need to create; but in its essence, immense and universal, it is impatient of working with lame or tied hands, and of making cripples and monsters, such as all pictures and statues are."[8] Therefore one must look upon the artist's works not with the "external eye" which sees only the crippling material "stuff," but with an inward vision that grasps the form of the ideal in the artist's mind. Hawthorne commented on the Christs and Madonnas of Francia: "His pictures are very singular and awkward, if you look at them with merely an external eye, but they are full of the beauty of holiness and evidently wrought out as acts of devotion, with the deepest sincerity; and are veritable prayers upon canvas" (X, 108). One is reminded of Emerson's indulgent praise of Ellery Channing's poetry: "Men of genius generally are, more than others, incapable of any perfect exhibition, because, however agreeable it may be to them to act on the public it is always a secondary aim. They are humble, self-accusing, moody men, whose worship is toward the Ideal Beauty, which chooses to be courted not so often in perfect hymns, as in wild, ear-piercing ejaculations or silent musings."[9] It is one of the amusing paradoxes of transcendentalism that Emerson and Hawthorne, conscientious and expert stylists both, should have given assent to a theory which made their own craft pointless.

What a work of art *suggested* was, after all, more significant than what it actually was. Hawthorne commented on the "Dying Gladiator," which he admired: "Like all other works of the highest excellence . . . it makes great demands upon the spectator; he must make a generous gift of his sympathies to the sculptor, and help out his skill with all his heart, or else he will see little more than a skillfully wrought surface. It suggests more than it shows" (X, 98). The high merit of such suggestiveness is expressed by Hilda in her response to Kenyon's wish that "his blurred and imperfect image" would make a respectable appearance in the eyes of those who had not seen the original: "There is a class of spectators whose sympathy will help them to see the perfect through a mist of imperfection. Nobody, I think, ought to read poetry, or look at pictures or statues, who cannot find a great deal more in them than the poet or artist has actually expressed. Their highest merit is suggestiveness" (VI, 431). The spectator must approach a work of art prepared to discover that its actual appearance also falls short of the ideal in *his* mind. When she finally views St. Peter's in Rome, Hilda finds that

> a shadowy edifice in her imagination had been dazzled out of sight by the reality. Her preconception of St. Peter's was a structure of no definite outline, misty in its architecture, dim and gray and huge, stretching into an interminable perspec-

tive, and overarched by a dome like the cloudy firmament. . . .
So, in her earlier visits, when the compassed splendor of the
actual interior glowed before her eyes, she had profanely
called it a great prettiness; a gay piece of cabinet-work, on a
Titanic scale; a jewel-casket, marvellously magnified (VI,
397).

In due time, Hilda feels that the great church does, indeed,
contain her dream of it. But it is only "after looking many
times, with long intervals between, [that] you discover that
the cathedral has gradually extended itself over the whole
compass of your visionary temple, and has room for its
cloudy pinnacles beneath the dome." (VI, 398).

The artist—or the true worshipper of art—would always
have a better vision in his mind than any he presented in
visible form to the world. Like Owen Warland,

> The poet leaves his song half sung, or finishes it, beyond the
> scope of mortal ears, in a celestial choir. The painter—as
> Allston did—leaves half his conception on the canvas to
> sadden us with its imperfect beauty, and goes to picture forth
> the whole, if it be no irreverence to say so, in the hues of
> heaven. But rather such incomplete designs of this life will
> be perfected nowhere. This so frequent abortion of man's
> dearest projects must be taken as a proof that the deeds of
> earth, however etherialized by piety or genius, are without
> value, except as exercises and manifestations of the spirit. In
> heaven, all ordinary thought is higher and more melodious
> than Milton's song (II, 526-27).

So, in the air castle of the Man of Fancy there stood along
the walls "a multitude of ideal statues, the original conceptions of the great works of ancient or modern art, which
the sculptors did but imperfectly succeed in putting into
marble" (II, 83), and he possessed a splendid library of
unwritten works, for "every author had imagined and
shaped out in his thought more and far better works than

those which actually proceeded from his own pen"—the untold tales of Chaucer's Canterbury pilgrims, the unwritten cantos of the *Faerie Queen,* Dryden's projected epic on the subject of King Arthur, and other such unrealized masterpieces. Sylph Etherege, seated at the window, is described as "a perfect picture; or, rather, it was like the original loveliness in a painter's fancy, from which the most finished picture is but an imperfect copy" (III, 508-9).

Hilda tells Kenyon:

> But you must not let yourself be too much disheartened by the decay of your faith in what you produce. I have heard a poet express similar disdain for his own most exquisite poem, and I am afraid that this final despair, and sense of short-coming, must always be the reward and punishment of those who try to grapple with a great and beautiful idea. It only proves you have been able to imagine things too high for mortal faculties to execute. The idea leaves you an imperfect image of itself, which you at first mistake for the real reality, but soon find that the latter has escaped out of your closest embrace (VI, 431).

We have seen how this dictum was the basis of Emerson's defense of his friend Channing's poetry (which Thoreau called "sublimo-slipshod"). To Channing himself, Emerson wrote:

> I prize at such dear rate the poetic soul, that where that is absent I can easily forgive the license and the negligence the absence of which makes the merit of mediocre verses; Nay, I do not know but I prefer the first draught and to be present at the secret of creation before the vamping and rhetoric are used which are but "the brushers of noblemen's clothes."[10]

This first draft of which Emerson speaks is an authentic Romantic symbol—the artist's first hasty sketch of what his inner eye has beheld, vague, suggestive, uncorrupted by the self-conscious, cramping hand of Fancy. Hawthorne repeatedly expressed this reverence for the sketch during his European travels. At the Louvre, for example, he reflected upon the pencil sketches of the masters:

> . . . the earliest drawing of their great pictures when they had the glory of their pristine idea directly before their mind's eye—that idea which inevitably became overlaid with their own handling of it, in the finished painting. No doubt the painters themselves had often a happiness in these rude, off-hand sketches, which they never felt again in the same work, and which resulted in disappointment after they had done their best (X, 27).

And, again, at the Uffizi, in Florence, he was moved to declare:

> [The sketches] certainly possess a charm that is lost in the finished picture; and I was more sensible of forecasting thought, skill, and prophetic design, in these sketches than in the most consummate works that have been elaborated from them. There is something more divine in these; for I suppose the first idea of a picture is real inspiration, and all the subsequent elaboration of the master serves but to cover up the celestial germ with something that belongs to himself (X, 397-8) .[11]

Was this enthusiasm for the sketch merely the result of the transcendental Sophia's unflagging instruction in the fine arts as she led Hawthorne from one European gallery to another? In *The Marble Faun* he observes that Miriam's workroom was "one of those delightful spots that hardly seem to belong to the actual world, but rather to be the outward type of a poet's haunted imagination, where there are glimpses, sketches, and half-developed hints of beings

and objects grander and more beautiful than we can anywhere find in reality" (VI, 57). It is plain that he also
regards the literary imagination in the light of this
Romantic principle. Romantic Platonism accounts for Hawthorne's conventional exaltation of the sketch, which sym-
bolizes for him the purest and most immediate response of
any sort of artist to his vision of the ideal. The sketch is a
graphic form of that language of natural passion which
Wordsworth spoke of as the poet's highest achievement.
The English Romantic poets, whatever their own procedure
in composition, preferred to conceive of the artist as the
vessel of inspiration, perfect only in its first irradiation; true
art, consequently, was the artist's unpremeditated and un-
mediated response to beauty—the *"spontaneous* overflow
of powerful feelings." Shelley's Platonic *Defence of Poetry*
expressed the matter most absolutely in its comparison of
the poet's mind to a fading coal:

> The mind in creation is as a coal, which some invisible in-
> fluence, like an inconstant wind, awakens to transitory
> brightness. . . . when composition begins, inspiration is al-
> ready on the decline, and the most glorious poetry that has
> ever been communicated to the world is probably a feeble
> shadow of the original conception of the poet.[12]

The sketch was valuable precisely because its lack of definition represented idea still unencased in conscious form.
Like Shelley, Hawthorne would seem to have approved

> aught that for its grace may be
> Dear, and yet dearer for its mystery.[13]

It may be noted that Hawthorne's Romantic disdain for
the physical form of finished art, his stated preference for
the inner essence, led not only to the exaltation of the sketch
but also to a special regard for ruins, which, besides their

other Romantic connotations, represented a reversion to the cloudy symbol of beauty first revealed in the mind of the architect. Furness Abbey, for example, exhibited to Hawthorne "a greater majesty and beauty than any human work can show—the crumbling traces of the half-obliterated design producing somewhat of the effect of the first idea of anything admirable, when it dawns upon the mind of an artist or a poet—an idea which, do what he may, he is sure to fall short of."[14]

We have seen how Hawthorne's express views of art seem to indicate that he often viewed aesthetic reality transcendentally. It will, then, not surprise us to find that he subscribes frequently to the Romantic view of artistic inspiration. When Hawthorne viewed the Venus de Medici in the Uffizi Gallery he remarked, "The sculptor must have wrought religiously, and have felt that something far beyond his own skill was working through his hands" (X, 303). This is the most ancient of all theories of artistic inspiration. The artist, a Caedmon or a Hesiod, is possessed by a power descending upon him from a heavenly source. Like Ion the rhapsodist, who, says Socrates, is actually ignorant of the rules of poetry, he effects a miracle beyond his own comprehension. So, when Hawthorne contemplated the Houses of Parliament from Westminster Bridge in 1855, he complained of a lack of impressiveness and declared that the architect had not, in Emerson's words, "builded better than he knew."[15] He had felt "no power higher and wiser than himself, making him its instrument; —he reckoned upon and contrived all his effects, with malice aforethought, and therefore missed the crowning effect —that being a happiness which God, out of his pure grace, mixes up with only the simple-hearted best efforts of men."[16]

To attain the height of inspiration, the Romantic artist must resemble the spiritualist medium or the religious

mystic. He cannot reach the heart of Nature by direct examination; rather, to his passive mind truth is suddenly
revealed by the flash of the imagination, the unsolicited
gift of grace. The beauty of Nature is, as Emerson had said,
"only a mirage as you look from the windows of dil-
igence."[17]

> I have before now experienced that the best way to get a vivid
> impression and feeling of a landscape is to sit down before it
> and read, or become otherwise absorbed in thought; for then,
> when your eyes happen to be attracted to the landscape, you
> seem to catch Nature at unawares,, and see her before she has
> time to change her aspect. The effect lasts but for a single
> instant, and passes away almost as soon as you are conscious
> of it; but it is real, for that moment. It is as if you could over-
> hear and understand what the trees are whispering to one
> another; as if you caught a glimpse of a face unveiled, which
> veils itself from every wilful glance. The mystery is revealed,
> and after a breath or two, becomes just as much a mystery as
> before.[18]

Art, also, must be viewed by the spectator in the same unpremeditated fashion. We have seen that Hilda found that
St. Peter's in Rome fell beneath her dim first imaginings
of it, and that she only recovered her early vision by repeated and separated revisits. Her experience, as we might
expect, was the novelist's own. Hawthorne had also found
his mind's St. Peter's destroyed by the sight of the real
building, but he found, too, that there was a way to recover
the splendor which had been taken from him. In his notebook observation he is more specific than in the novel,
prescribing the casual glance that allows for inspired in-
tuition, instead of studied scrutiny, as the remedy.

> At times, a single, casual, momentary glimpse of its magnifi-
> cence gleams upon my soul, as it were, when I happen to

glance at arch opening beyond arch, and I am surprised into admiration. I have experienced that a landscape and the sky unfold the deepest beauty in a similar way; not when they are gazed at of set purpose, but when the spectator looks suddenly through a vista, among a crowd of other thoughts (X, 88).[19]

Of a painting of Hope by Guido, Hawthorne wrote that

it has a grace which artists are continually trying to get into their innumerable copies, but always without success; for, indeed, though nothing is more true than the existence of this charm in the picture, yet if you try to analyze it, or even look too intently at it, it vanishes, till you look again with more trusting simplicity (X, 165).

This transcendental "submission of the will" to the current of the invisible is the Romantic version of the phenomenon of poetic inspiration. Emerson wrote, for example, that the poet must give up his individuality in surrender to the current of nature. The imagination, he wrote,

exists by sharing the ethereal currents. The poet contemplates the central identity, sees it undulate and roll this way and that, with divine flowings, through remotest things; and, following it, can detect essential resemblances in natures never before compared. He can class them so audaciously because he is sensible of the sweep of the celestial stream, from which nothing is exempt. His own body is a fleeing apparition,—his personality as fugitive as the hope it employs ... he knows that he did not make his thought, no—his thought made him, and made the sun and stars.[20]

The ability to create works of art was not so much dependent upon an innate capacity which dwells in each soul, its heritage from a former state, unrealized unless awakened by some superior force. "In every human spirit," Hawthorne remarks in "Drowne's Wooden Image, "there is imagination, sensibility, creative power, genius, which, according to circumstances, may either be developed, in this world, or shrouded in a mask of dulness until another state of being" (II, 362).

Yet paradoxically, and, again, like his Romantic contemporaries, Hawthorne seems to have given assent to the gospel of the artist's supremacy, his *unique* power to see into the heart of things. Sophia was wont to think of her husband as a "heaven-gifted seer,"[21] and while it is difficult to imagine Hawthorne describing himself in such supernal terms, he was undoubtedly influenced by the contemporary apotheosis of the poet as prophet and hero, "unacknowledged legislator" and inspired miracle-worker, which was to be met with in the work of the Romantic writers. When visiting Stanton Harcourt, where Pope had lived while translating the *Iliad,* and having just previously seen Blenheim, he was moved to remark:

> A poet has a fragrance about him, such as no other human being is gifted withal; it is indestructible, and clings for evermore to everything that he has touched. I was not impressed, at Blenheim, with any sense that the mighty Duke still haunted the palace that was created for him; but here, after a century and a half, we are still conscious of the presence of that decrepit little figure of Queen Anne's time, although he was merely a casual guest in the old tower, during one or two summer months (VII, 223).

The poet was like no other man; his gift to life was that of eternity.

> We neither remember nor care anything for the past, except as the poet has made it intelligibly noble and sublime to our comprehension. The shades of the mighty have no substance; they flit ineffectually about the darkened stage where they

performed their momentary parts, save when the poet has thrown his own creative soul into them, and imparted a more vivid life than even they were able to manifest to mankind while they dwelt in the body. And therefore—though he cunningly disguises himself in their armor, their robes of state, or kingly purple—it is not the stateman, the warrior, or the monarch that survives, but the despised poet, whom they may have fed with their crumbs, and to whom they owe all that they now are or have,—a name! (VII, 315-16).

The works of the divinely inspired artist are, naturally, themselves of a supernatural order—magical works. Of his favorite, Guido's "Cenci," Hawthorne said, "Its spell is indefinable and the painter has wrought it in a way more like magic than anything else I have known" (X, 89). While he was having his portrait painted by C. G. Thompson in 1850, Hawthorne confided to his notebook: "I love the odor of paint in an artist's room; his palette and all his other tools have a mysterious charm for me. The pursuit has always interested my imagination more than any other, and I remember before having my first portrait taken, there was a great bewitchery in the idea as if it was a magic process" (IX, 373-74).[22] He felt that painting, more than any other art, possessed this nearly supernatural power. "It is my present opinion that the pictorial art is capable of something more like magic—more wonderful and inscrutable in its methods than poetry, or any other mode of developing the beautiful" (X, 300).

But literature also was capable of the same wonder-working. In the *Mosses* he declared that he had "a superstitious reverence for literature of all kinds," and that he hoped that each book he read contained "the spell to disclose treasures in some unsuspected cave of truth" (II, 31).

In the preceding pages we have observed that Hawthorne expresses the view that art is a presentation of the ideal that

lies behind the curtain of the visible world. He seems to
have given assent to the superior reality of spiritual over
material events, regarding the world of facts as the "garb of
external circumstances." The artist is able to glimpse this
superior reality in moments of inspiration which are outside our ordinary experience. His vision is most intense at
the moment of illumination; then, "like a fading coal," his
knowledge of the truth of the spirit dims in the intellectual
afterthought of conscious art. Hence, what is important in
a work of art is not the superficies that satisfy the external
senses, but the hint of original inspiration. The imperfect
sketch may be closer to the soul of the artist than the
finished masterpiece. The true artist is a vessel of higher
powers, and more often achieves his best results by a "wise
passiveness" to these unseen influences than by deliberate
efforts of the mind. The artistic act is "the bond of union
with the Giver," a lesser manifestation of divine creativeness; its products have miraculous properties.

The various strands of viewpoint assembled above cohere
easily under the general title of transcendentalism, which
Hoxie N. Fairchild defined as a "belief in the dominance of
the intuitive and spiritual elements of mentality over sense
experience."[23] As Professor Fairchild pointed out, the
transcendentalism of the Romantics was poetic rather than
formally philosophical, as appears in their fondness for
drawing analogies between the transcendental faculty of
the Reason and the creative imagination of the artist. In
the transcendental aesthetic, Imagination is opposed to
Fancy across the same axis that separates the Reason from
the Understanding, and the moral activity of the "Heart"
from that of the "Head." There is no question, as we have
seen, that Hawthorne gave considerable assent to the usual
Romantic ordination of the artist, which depended philo-
sophically upon the superior status of Reason, Imagination,
and intuitive impulse. We shall later have occasion to note

that all six terms play a part in Hawthorne's creative speculation, particularly in the story "The Artist of the Beautiful," which I shall analyze in detail. Nevertheless, though
Hawthorne's use of the polarities of Head and Heart often
provides the cross-tensions of his fiction, we shall discover
that he has, actually, manipulated the terms critically to
serve his own ends. And though the antonymous pairs
Reason and Understanding and Imagination and Fancy
appear to have supported his aesthetic, we shall have subsequent occasion to discover that he is critical of the *effect*
of these ideas, if not of their philosophic formulation.

The identification of the transcendental faculty of Reason
with the poetic imagination was one that Hawthorne absorbed to an evident degree. It was, one may note, *all there
was to absorb* in the way of current aesthetic philosophy—
the prevailing intellectual mode of his time. Stemming
from Kant's well-known distinction between the *Verstand*
and *Vernuft,* popularized by Coleridge (whose *Aids to Reflection* was published by James Marsh at Burlington, Ver-
mont, in 1829), the Reason-Understanding antithesis became the stock philosophic formula of American intellectuals during the thirties and forties. In 1834 Emerson
wrote his brother:

Philosophy affirms that the outward world is only phenome-
nal & the whole concern of dinners of tailors of gigs of balls
whereof men make such account is a quite relative & temporary one—an intricate dream—the exhalation of the present
state of the Soul—wherein the Understanding works inces-
santly as if it were real but the eternal Reason when now &
then he is allowed to speak declares it is an accident a smoke
nowise related to his permanent attributes. . . . Now that I
have used the words, let me ask you do you draw the distinction of Milton Coleridge & the Germans between Reason &
Understanding. I think it is philosophy itself & like all truth
very practical.[24]

Now, to Kant, as is well known, Reason and Understanding were faculties which operated without prejudice to one another to secure knowledge of distinct spheres of being. But Romantic transcendentalism was to exalt the first instrument of the mind and degrade the second.[25] And Emerson and the English Romantics went on to define imagination as a quality identical with Reason, "another name for absolute power/And clearest insight, amplitude of mind,/And reason in her most exalted mood."[26] It was this identification that gave the artist a philosophical, even a religious, dignity. The Romantics were confident that the imagination was somehow concerned with insight into a supernatural order. This was undoubtedly the formula which Hawthorne absorbed almost unconsciously from the general ambiance of transcendentalism in which he lived and worked as an artist. That he was also critical of the consequences of an unnatural and perhaps even dangerous exaltation of the artist remains to be seen. But much of the structure still stands intact after the criticism has done its work.

The distinction between Imagination and Fancy, which is probably the part of the Romantic aesthetic that still seems employable to us, seemed sound as a practical mode of aesthetic discrimination to Hawthorne also. We have already noted that Hawthorne condemned works which aimed merely to please the eye, not the soul. It is Fancy which achieves the satisfaction of the external senses. And Fancy had been responsible for the "Sonnet to the Snow on Mount Washington," written by the young poet in the early "Sketches from Memory."

> The lines were elegant and full of fancy, but too remote from familiar sentiment, and cold as their subject, resembling those curious specimens of crystallized vapor which I observed next day on the mountain top (II, 481).

But the poet in "The Great Stone Face" is a votary of the Imagination:

> This man of genius, we may say, had come down from heaven with wonderful endowments. If he sang of a mountain, the eyes of all mankind beheld a mightier grandeur reposing on its breast, or soaring to its summit, than had before been seen there. If his theme were a lovely lake, a celestial smile had now been thrown over it, to gleam forever on its surface. If it were the vast old sea, even the deep immensity of its dread bosom seemed to swell the higher, as if moved by the emotions of the song. Thus the world assumed another and a better aspect from the hour that the poet blessed it with his happy eyes. The Creator had bestowed him, as the last best touch to his own handiwork. Creation was not finished till the poet came to interpret, and so complete it (III, 432-33).

During his European travels, Hawthorne's observations on art evinced his desire to distinguish between the products of Imagination and Fancy. The extreme literalist detail of the Pre-Raphaelites struck him as being the accomplishment of Fancy. He disliked a painting of Millais, representing the parting of two lovers, which he saw in Manchester, because

> an old brick wall, over-run with foliage, was so exquisitely and elaborately wrought, that it was hardly possible to look at the personages of the picture. Every separate leaf of the climbing and clustering shrubbery was painfully made out; and the wall was reality itself, with the weatherstains, and the moss, and the crumbling lime between the bricks. It is not well to be so perfect in the inanimate, unless the artist can likewise make man and woman as lifelike—and to as great a depth too—as the Creator does.[27]

In Italy, Hawthorne repeatedly rejected the art which seemed to him to be the work of Fancy. As we have seen previously, he often stated that painting must do more than merely please the senses; it must suggest a vital wholeness, a living soul. The American portrait painter William Page, Hawthorne was told, had taken seventy-three sittings to complete a portrait of Browning. "In the result, every hair and speck of him was represented; yet . . . this accumulation of minute truths did not, after all, amount to the true whole" (X, 336). In 1858, when he visited the studio of Thomas Crawford in Rome, he dismissed the artist's works as "commonplaces in marble and plaster," and observed particularly of a grandiose portrait-statue of Washington, "It does not impress me as having grown out of any genuine idea in the artist's mind, but being merely an ingenious contrivance enough" (X, 124). Perhaps the most redoubtable champion of Fancy whom Hawthorne encountered was Hiram Powers. Hawthorne described Powers—who thought the head of the Venus de Milo ill-proportioned, and who explained that the effectiveness of Michaelangelo's portrait-bust of Lorenzo de Medici was produced by the shadow cast onto the face by the helmet—as "seeing too clearly what is within his range to be aware of any region of mystery beyond" (X, 335).[28]

The whole problem of Imagination versus Fancy is treated with some elaborateness in *The Marble Faun*. The chapter titled "An Aesthetic Company" introduces in thin disguise most of the artistic acquaintances Hawthorne made in Italy—John Gibson, Cephas Giovanni Thompson, George Loring Brown, Thomas Buchanan Read, and Hiram Powers.[29] Still other American artists are mentioned and discussed in the book—William Wetmore Story, Paul Akers, Randolph Rogers, Harriet Hosmer, Horatio Greenough, and Thomas Crawford. Hawthorne was interested in the aesthetic problems posed by these artists' varying styles, seeing them chiefly in terms of the Imagination-Fancy antithesis. Gibson, whose tobacco-colored Venuses aroused Miriam's scorn (VI, 149), may be taken as Hawthorne's representative portrait of the artist of Fancy. "One sculptor there was, an Englishman, endowed with a beautiful fancy, and possessing at his fingers' ends the capability of doing beautiful things. . . . He had spent his life, for forty years, in making Venuses, Cupids, Bacchuses, and a vast deal of other marble progeny of dream-work, or rather frost-work . . ." (VI, 161). On the other hand, an artist who has been identified as George L. Brown was described as one "who has studied Nature with such tender love that she takes him to her intimacy, enabling him to reproduce her in landscapes that seem the reality of a better earth, and yet are but the truth of the very scenes around us, observed by the painter's insight and interpreted for us by his skill." And a poet-painter, who is undoubtedly meant to be Thomas B. Read, is one "whose song has the vividness of picture, and whose canvas is peopled with angels, fairies, and water-sprites, done to the ethereal life, because he saw them face to face in his poetic mood." Hawthorne urges us finally to bow before one "who has wrought too sincerely, too religiously, with too earnest a feeling, and too delicate a touch, for the world at once to recognize how much toil and thought are compressed" into his work (VI, 160-61).

Reviewing the sculptors of the "aesthetic company," Hawthorne distinguishes between the artists of fancy and those of true imagination:

> It is fair to say that they were a body of very dexterous and capable artists, each of whom had probably given the delighted public a nude statue, or had won credit for even higher skill by the nice carving of button-holes, shoe-ties, coat-seams, shirt-bosoms, and other such graceful peculiarities of modern costume. Smart, practical men they doubtless were, and some of them far more than this, but, still, not precisely what an uninitiated person looks for in a sculptor. A

sculptor, indeed, to meet the demands which our preconceptions make upon him, should be even more indispensably a poet than those who deal in measured verse and rhyme. His material, or instrument, which serves him in the stead of shifting and transitory language, is a pure, white, undecaying substance. It insures immortality to whatever is wrought in it, and therefore makes it a religious obligation to commit no idea to its mighty guardianship save such as may repay the marble for its faithful care, its incorruptible fidelity, by warming it with an ethereal life. Under this aspect, marble assumes a sacred character; and no man should dare to touch it unless he feels within himself a certain consecration and a priesthood, the only evidence of which, for the public eye, will be the high treatment of heroic subjects, or the delicate evolution of spiritual, through material beauty (VI, 162-63).

THE SYMBOLIC MIRROR OF ART

In the following chapters I shall examine Hawthorne's view of the artist as it emerges from his complex imaginative designs, and will disclose a figure quite opposed to the artist-hero who has come into view above. Yet this second figure at times gives way, in the fiction, to the transcendental poet-seer, for Hawthorne's feelings never quite swept away his wistful desire that the artist might indeed be all the Romantics claimed. In the end, though his most deeply felt image of the artist was that of a worker of illicit black magic, he sometimes glimpsed the gentler figure whose "white" art achieved true miracles through its source in the divine. It was to this second, happier, portrait of the artist that much of his conscious assent, at any rate, was given, as the preceding pages have shown.

One minor, but persistent, image represents the transcendental strain in Hawthorne's writing, and may serve to conclude our examination of this element in his aesthetic theory. In mirrors, and in reflections of all sorts, as both F. O. Matthiessen and Malcolm Cowley have noted,[30] Hawthorne often amused himself by imagining that he saw the realm of the ideal. So, boating along the quiet North Branch of the Concord River, he gazed with transcendental rapture at the mirrored scene:

I have never elsewhere had such an opportunity to observe how much more beautiful reflection is than what we call reality. The sky, and the clustering foliage on either hand, and the effect of sunlight as it found its way through the shade, giving lightsome hues in contrast with the quiet depth of the prevailing tints—all these seemed unsurpassably beautiful, when beheld in the upper air. But, on gazing downward, there they were, the same even to the minutest particular, yet arrayed in ideal beauty, which satisfied the spirit incomparably more than the actual scene. I am half convinced that the reflection is indeed the reality—the real thing which Nature imperfectly images to our grosser sense. At all events, the disembodied shadow is nearest to the soul.[31]

The mirror-image in the smooth surface of the water may also be Hawthorne's symbol for the imagination, which, "reflecting" nature, does more than reflect—opens like a window into the invisible world of real forms. "The reflection is indeed the reality," says Hawthorne, and, conversely, the actual scene is but a reflection of an invisible reality. As Blake wrote, "There exist in that Eternal world the Permanent Realities of Everything which we see reflected in this Vegetable Glass of Nature."[32]

The comparison of art to a mirror originates, of course, as a deprecation. If what the artist does is merely to depict or reflect what he sees in Blake's "Vegetable Glass of Nature" he produces only that poor thing, Plato's third bed —the dim copy of the carpenter's shadow of that Eternal Bed which is the Divine Idea. With Aristotle, however, and for centuries after, "imitation" became the inevitable term to describe—and approve—the artist's function. And for this mimetic art a constant symbol, right through the eighteenth century, was the mirror. Though neoclassic aesthetics often affirmed that the artist *selected* the typical and true from the spectacle of the natural and human world, the aesthetic image was still described as a kind of reflection; it took its qualities and forms from the reality known to the senses. M. H. Abrams, in his summary of Romantic critical theory, *The Mirror and the Lamp*,[33] thus contrasts the mirror as a neoclassical "metaphor of mind" with the lamp, a radiant source more apt to describe the Romantic conception of the "creative" imagination.

And yet could not the mirror image, adapted to the Plotinian rather than the Platonic explanation of the artist's activity, be used also to represent the mind as a looking glass which one could both see into and go through, like Alice? What might be seen in this looking glass was not the sensible world at all, and did not derive from it, but the Ideas residing in that heaven of Pure Forms from which the physical world also more imperfectly derives. Such a magic mirror would disclose the truth otherwise hidden from men; one could see through it into a sacred and eternal Nature. It became a precious entrance, Keats' "magic casement." Such is the mirror of art in Hawthorne's aesthetics.

Both Hawthorne's American and European *Notebooks* abound in references to mirrors, pools, and reflecting surfaces. Hawthorne was always taking a quick glance at the spectral world beyond a reflection, the image, which, purged of matter, was the symbol of the thought expressed by Emerson when he said, "The laws of moral nature answer those of matter as face to face in a glass."[34]

As early as 1835 Hawthorne notes the sight of the reflection in the North River with grave attention (IX, 23), and the following year the remark occurs, "No fountain so small but that heaven may be imaged in its bosom" (IX, 37). Years later, during his travels in France and Italy, he records in his notebook that he glanced with curiosity at himself in Catherine de Medici's dressing glass; in the fountain of Trevi tried to imagine Corinne's image as seen by Lord Neville; at Arezzo stopped at a well dating back to Boccaccio's time and looked down through the opening in the wooden cover to see his own face where Boccaccio might have looked to see his; and in Florence, in the Chapel of the Annunziata, found a well which fascinated him: "The surface of the water lay deep within the deepest dust of dead people and thence threw up its picture of the sky" (I, 18, 205, 326, 451).

Sometimes it is another and more mysterious self that seems to beckon from the silent reflecting surface. "From my childhood I have loved to gaze into a spring," says the narrator of "The Vision of the Fountain" (I, 242), and "Monsieur du Miroir" spins out to the point of tedium the idea of a spectral double who forever accompanies one in the mirrors of this world. Like many "double" stories— Poe's "William Wilson" and Conrad's "The Secret Sharer," for example—"Monsieur du Miroir" may express, however unprofoundly, a sense of psychological depths beneath the surface of behavior and even of consciousness. Malcolm Cowley concludes from such examples that the chief significance of Hawthorne's interest in the image of the mirror is biographically psychological; the images are, he feels, revelations of Hawthorne's personal "doubleness" and of a strain of narcissism that developed him from a beautiful, petted boy into a man morbidly self-absorbed and torpid. But such a genesis for the mirror image seems to me less important, even if, possibly, true, than the evolution of its meaning as a representation of the transcendental view of art. Hawthorne was more than likely to translate such an intimation of personal and private meaning into philosophic terms, to conclude that the hidden soul was part of the world-soul. And so these images came to represent, as Matthiessen noted, symbolic apertures into the universal mind of which the Romantics were so fond of talking.[35] In this way they are appropriate symbols of the poetic imagination, which has unique access to a vision of eternity, of past and future. That is why the mirrors in "Old Esther Dudley" and "Dr. Heidigger's Experiment" were reputed to be inhabited by the ghosts of people long dead (I, 334, 259), and why, as Phoebe and Holgrave leave the House of the Seven Gables for the last time, Maule's well, "though left in solitude, was throwing up a succession of kaleidoscopic pictures, in which a gifted eye might have foreshadowed the coming fortunes of Hepzibah and Clifford" (III, 377).

Again, the mirrors in "Feathertop" and "Dr. Heidigger's Experiment" show not what the external eye is tricked by, but the truth, the essence. As Dr. Heidigger's rejuvenated old friends cavort before it, "the tall mirror is said to have reflected the figures of three old, gray, withered grandsires ridiculously contending for the skinny ugliness of a shrivelled grandam" (I, 268-69). And as Feathertop struts his hollow elegance before Polly, she catches sight of him in the full-length looking glass, "one of the truest plates in the world, and incapable of flattery," seeing there "not the glittering mockery of his outward show, but a picture of the sordid patchwork of his real composition" (II, 276). Such a truth-telling mirror is the image Hawthorne uses to describe Chillingworth's belated insight into the transformation that his own character has undergone during his persecution of Arthur Dimmesdale. Though to all others he seems unchanged, Chillingworth suddenly glimpses his true aspect and lifts his hands in horror, Hawthorne says, "as if he had beheld some frightful shape which he could not recognize, usurping the place of his own image in a glass" (V, 207).

Hawthorne sums up the symbolic attributes of his mirrors in *The House of the Seven Gables* in that chapter in which the dead judge sits for a world-portrait by moonlight.

As the eerie scene reveals itself in the glass, Hawthorne observes that a mirror "is always a kind of window or doorway into the spiritual world" (III, 332). Such a window, he sometimes seemed to believe, was art. The same conjunction of mirror and moonlight is invoked by him again, in "The Custom House," the "introductory sketch" which Hawthorne attached to *The Scarlet Letter*, to represent the power of the imagination to reveal the deeper, spiritual truth of things.

In this whimsical and yet profoundly suggestive and self-communing essay, Hawthorne remarks: "Glancing at the looking-glass, we behold—deep within its haunted verge —the smouldering glow of the half-extinguished anthracite, the white moonbeams on the floor, and a repetition of all the gleam and shadow of the picture, with one remove further from the actual, and nearer to the imagination. Then, at such an hour, and with this scene before him, if a man, sitting all alone, cannot dream strange things, and make them look like truth, he need never try to write romances" (V, 56). Every bit of this is suggestive—the mirror as the entry into a "haunted" realm, a realm of a supernatural reality; the mirror which receives into its bosom the impalpable essence, the "gleam and shadow" of the visible world, bringing it closer to the real, freeing it from the actual; finally, the imagination, which the mirror of art must reflect if the artist would hope to write romances.

In the mirror of the artistic imagination, as Hawthorne conceived it, actuality became ideality, yet he was seldom able to feel, as we shall see, that he had successfully achieved this Romantic miracle. In the *Scarlet Letter* introduction, he goes on to declare that his own imagination had proved but "a tarnished mirror" because it could not extract spiritual truth from the dingy substance of the Salem Custom House. And perhaps he was never to be satisfied that his imagination was capable of such happy transformations.

For Hawthorne regarded the claims of the earthly half of existence, of solid earth and human flesh, as equally worthy with those of the spirit. His art is rooted in a denial of the right of either to exploit the other.

NOTES TO CHAPTER II

[1] Quoted in *Hawthorne* by Newton Arvin (Boston: Little, Brown and Co., 1929) , p. 92.

[2] *Ibid.,* p. 91.

[3] "Hawthorne: A Puritan Critic of Puritanism," *Americans* (New York: Charles Scribner's Sons, 1922) , pp. 126-27.

[4] Quoted, as are the next two passages, from Mrs. Hawthorne's version of the *American Notebooks.* Since no manuscript original survives for these entries, they are not reproduced in Stewart's edition. They may, therefore, still include some traces of her revising hand; perhaps, one may speculate, some qualifying anti-transcendentalism may have been removed by her at this point.

[5] *The English Notebooks by Nathaniel Hawthorne,* ed. Randall Stewart (New York, 1941) , p. 549. All references to Hawthorne's *English Notebooks* will be to this edition, which has replaced Mrs. Hawthorne's emended text.

[6] *Ibid.,* p. 550.

[7] *The Flowering of New England* (New York: E. P. Dutton and Co., 1936) , p. 475.

[8] "Art," *Works,* II, 362, 363.

[9] "The New Poetry," *The Dial,* I (October, 1840) , 222-32. Cited in *The Transcendentalists,* ed. Perry Miller (Cambridge, Mass.: Harvard University Press, 1950) , p. 377.

[10] To W. E. Channing, Concord, January, 1840, *Letters of Ralph Waldo Emerson,* ed. Ralph Rusk (New York: Columbia University Press, 1939) , II, 253.

[11] See also *The Marble Faun,* VI, 165-66; *English Notebooks,* p. 414; Julian Hawthorne, *Hawthorne and His Wife,* II, 187-88.

[12] "Defence of Poetry," *The Complete Works of Percy Bysshe Shelley,* ed. R. Ingpen and W. E. Peck (London and New York: Ernest Benn Limited; Charles Scribner's Sons, 1926-30) , VII, 135.

[13] "Hymn to Intellectual Beauty," *ibid.,* II, 60.

[14] *English Notebooks,* p. 157.

[15] "The Problem," *Works,* IX, 7, line 23.

[16] *English Notebooks,* p. 249.

[17] "Nature," *Works,* I, 25.

[18] *American Notebooks,* pp. 241-42. Cf. *ibid.,* p. 199; *English Notebooks,* pp. 333-34.

[19] Cf. *The Marble Faun,* VI, 371.

[20] "Poetry and Imagination," *Works,* VIII, 21, 39.

[21] Stewart, *Nathaniel Hawthorne,* p. 81.

[22] Another passage available only in Mrs. Hawthorne's version of the *American Notebooks,* since it was scissored (with what discordant additions, one may wonder) from the Morgan manuscript, upon which Stewart's edition is based.

[23] *The Romantic Quest* (New York: Columbia University Press, 1931) , p. 141.

[24] Emerson, *Letters,* I, 412-13.

[25] Coleridge called the Reason "best and holiest gift of God and bond of union with the giver; the high title by which the majesty of man claims precedence over all other living creatures—mysterious faculty, the mother of conscience ... calm and incorruptible legislator of the soul, sole principle of permanence amid endless change" (*The Friend,* ed. H. N. Coleridge [London: W. Pickering, 1937], I, 259-60) . Carlyle exalted the higher faculty as "the pure, ultimate light of our nature; where ... lies the foundation of all Poetry, Virtue, Religion, things which are properly beyond the province of the Understanding" ("State of German Literature," *The Works of Thomas Carlyle,* ed. H. D. Traill [Centenary ed.; London: Chapman and Hall, 1896-1901], XXVI, 81-83) .

[26] Wordsworth, *The Prelude,* Book XIV.

[27] *English Notebooks,* p. 352.

[28] In 1849, William Wetmore Story wrote Lowell that he thought Powers to be "a man of great mechanical talent and natural strength of perception, but with no poetry in his composition and I think no creative power" (Henry James, *William Wetmore Story and His Friends* [Boston: Houghton, Mifflin and Co., 1903], I, 172) . It is possible that Hawthorne borrowed his opinion of Powers from Story, whom he was seeing at the time.

[29] I am indebted for these identifications to Norman Holmes Pearson, of Yale University, whose unpublished edition of Hawthorne's *French and Italian Notebooks* (Ph.D. dissertation, Yale, 1942) provides valuable annotation to *The Marble Faun.*

[30] F. O. Matthiessen, *American Renaissance* (New York: Oxford

University Press, 1941) , pp. 259-62; *The Portable Hawthorne,* ed. with an Introduction by Malcolm Cowley (New York: The Viking Press, 1948) , pp. 8-9.

[31] *American Notebooks,* p. 170. See also p. 148, and "The Old Manse" (II, 32) .

[32] "A Vision of the Last Judgment," *Poetry and Prose of William Blake,* ed. Geoffrey Keynes (London: The Nonesuch Press, 1939) , p. 639.

[33] New York: Oxford University Press, 1953.

[34] "Nature," *Works,* I, 32-33.

[35] *American Renaissance,* p. 260.

[36] Shelley had written in his neo-Platonic "Defence of Poetry": "A story of particular facts is as a mirror which obscures and distorts that which should be beautiful; poetry is a mirror which makes beautiful that which is distorted." *Works,* VII, 115.

Chapter III

Anti-Romantic Patterns in Hawthorne's Fiction

~~~~~~~~~~~~~~~~~~~~~~~~~~~~~~~~~~~~~

It is the time when uprightly and in pious sober wise, naught of work is to be wrought and art grown impossible without the devil's help and fires of hell under the cauldron.
—THOMAS MANN, *Dr. Faustus*

Despite the evidence exhibited in the previous chapter, the transcendental view of the artist represents only part of Hawthorne's thinking on the subject, and actually its less vital part—a sort of passive residue which in his art he seems continually to struggle against. It is no accident that the evidence of another side comes hardly at all from random remark and comment but almost entirely from the inner themes of Hawthorne's fiction. These inner themes comprise not the conscious aesthetics of a man who was an unoriginal and unselftaxing theorist, but the emotion inescapably present in all his imaginings about artists. They show us Hawthorne at his most profound and personal, the Hawthorne who felt no obligation to be respectful of the opinions of his Concord neighbors, but expressed his most troubling and penetrating ideas through allegory.

As observed earlier, Hawthorne found the Romantic tradition itself of some help in this struggle. He was, to employ

Peckham's formula, a "negative Romantic." Thus, he found at hand in an alternative Romantic strain the melancholy artist-figure who, far from being hailed as a seer by his fellow man, was regarded as an outcast, if not as a criminal. Young Fanshawe, we shall see, is clearly of this type. He is the familiar *poète maudit*, the unhappy genius doomed to live unloved and die young. Less obviously, but just as certainly, Owen Warland, the hero of "The Artist of the Beautiful," is brother to the great nineteenth-century company of real and fictional beautiful souls who live misunderstood by the coarser spirits of the world, and seek an early grave—Chatterton and Werther, Henry Kirke White and Clare's "Village Minstrel"—the type has been often catalogued. The Byronic hero included the ingredient of secret guilt in his burden of sorrows—and there may be traces of this type in Hawthorne's painter of "The Prophetic Pictures," in Roderick Elliston and Ethan Brand, and perhaps in the ministers Hooper and Dimmesdale, who all have "self-condemning bosoms," like Childe Harold.[1]

I have shown evidence of Hawthorne's interest in the transcendental doctrine of artistic inspiration, which attributed the powers of the artist to a divine source. From ancient times, however, there existed the suspicion that the artist's inspiration could come from below as well as from above, just as the medieval ghost could be either a heavenly visitant or a devil leading one into an abyss. Even Emerson was moved to declare that he might be the Devil's child. The idealist seeker of eternal truths is flanked in Romantic thought by the necromantic Faustian figure who has bartered for knowledge with his soul. In Romantic Gothicism, we find the sinister twin of the ordained artist of Emerson and the English Romantics, a Magian figure whose knowledge is chthonian and whose works represent an illicit black magic. Hawthorne's artists, as well as his scholars and scientists, have a much closer relation to the Gothic figure of the evil necromancer than to the artist-ideal who emerges in the quotations just surveyed. Like Faust, they seem to demonstrate that the power of knowledge which rivals God's own can work not only good, but harm. They practice an occultism which is the dark side of the Romantic quest, a criticism of it, perhaps, and not merely Gothic gooseflesh. In the same tradition, Hawthorne found the symbol of the magic art-object, a favorite device in the horror novels of Walpole and Mrs. Radcliffe. Hawthorne responded to this theme when he wrote "The Prophetic Pictures," just as did Poe in "The Oval Portrait," or Gogol in "The Mysterious Portrait." We shall look later at the similarities existing among these contemporary stories. Poe and Gogol, like Hawthorne, would seem to have been struck by a fresh expressive potentiality in the demoniacally magical work of art.

It has been generally observed that Hawthorne was attracted by the Gothic novel, and his work is replete with the trappings and stock themes to be found in the "haunted castle" literature so popular in his day.[2] But, as Paul Elmer More pointed out, Hawthorne was a Gothic artist with a difference, using the same machinery as the German and English horror writers, but speaking from the profound moral depths of his time and country.[3] Thus, he never—except in his weakest moments—uses the Gothic material for its own sake. We will see how a number of Gothic motifs—purely "thriller" ingredients in the hands of inferior writers—have a relation to his view of the artist.

The theme of the elixir of perpetual life, for example, is curiously intertwined with Hawthorne's ponderings concerning the relation of human striving—such as the artist's—to the limitations imposed by Nature. In "A Virtuoso's Collection" (II, 551-52) and "The Birthmark" (II, 58), he condemned the hope that human life might be infinitely prolonged, but in "The Artist of the Beautiful" he was moved to observe that an artist might find one lifetime inadequate in which to accomplish his aim (II, 526). In the unfinished romances that occupied Hawthorne after his return from England, he took up the theme again, attempting to build at least two full-length novels about the story of

> a man of high purposes, which he hates to leave unaccomplished. This nostrum to bring back his youth is a thing to which he otherwise attaches no importance. He knows that it is inconsistent with the plan of the world, and, if generally adopted, would throw everything into confusion; he therefore considers it justifiable only in his own exceptional case.[4]

We shall see further on that Septimius Felton is one of Hawthorne's artist types. In his desire for a magic elixir he expresses the same impulse to get outside the human sphere which Hawthorne felt to be dangerous in the artist. He craves such knowledge concerning human events as is not normally granted to men. It is the kind of knowledge Ethan Brand wanted, the blighting wisdom granted the painter of "The Prophetic Pictures." Septimius would obtain it by an infinite amplitude of personal experience. He might, for example, spend a century being wicked, he tells Sibyl Dacy:

> How can I know my brethren unless I do that once? I would experience all. Imagination is only a dream. I can imagine myself a murderer, and all other modes of crime; but it leaves no real impression on the heart. I must live these things (XI, 409).

So Septimius is not unlike the novel writer referred to in "Fancy's Show Box" who "in order to produce a sense of reality in the reader's mind" must conceive a train of incidents or a villain of romance so "as to seem, in the glow of fancy, more like truth, past, present, or to come, than purely fiction." By so doing, artist and villain become identified. "Thus a novel writer or a dramatist, in creating a villain of romance and fitting him with evil deeds, and the villain of actual life, in projecting crimes that will be perpetrated, may almost meet each other half-way between reality and fancy" (I, 256).

The theme of perpetual life is also related to the ancient story of the Wandering Jew, which, in 1845, Hawthorne speculated upon as a possible subject for a story.[5] The Wandering Jew, like Cain and Ishmael, had a curious appeal for the mind of the nineteenth-century artist as a symbolic example of the condition of guilt and isolation which seemed to be his own. Yet none of the many writers who were haunted by the legend seem to have been able to make what they wanted of it. It interested Goethe and Shelley—as it did Hawthorne, who first experimented with this enigmatic figure in the early sketch "A Virtuoso's Collection" and was still trying to put it to use in *Septimius Felton*—but it remained the property of the Gothic novelists Godwin and Lewis, as a piece of Romantic machinery.[6] Byron's Cain, Coleridge's Ancient Mariner, and Melville's Ishmael show how deeply these artists felt the general theme of the outcast. And this theme may be said to be Hawthorne's chief preoccupation as a writer and one which he identified with the artist's situation.

Goethe, we know, gave up the theme of the Wandering Jew in favor of a poetic work based on the parallel legend of Faust. *Faust*, of course, is the great example of Romantic machinery turned upon itself: the Gothic Faust figure becomes a profound criticism of the religion of infinite striving. In a sense, Hawthorne's work bears the imprint of a similar process.[7] Rappaccini, Ethan Brand, and Aylmer are Faustian figures who in their lust for superhuman knowledge and power barter their humanity. Of Dr. Rappaccini, his rival, Baglioni, declares: "He would sacrifice human life, his own among the rest, or whatever else was dearest to him, for the sake of adding so much as a grain of mustard seed to the great heap of his accumulated knowledge" (II, 116). Brand, who began his search for the unpardonable sin after many nightly conferences with a fiend evoked from the furnace of his limekiln, surrenders himself to the consuming fire of the kiln, which claims him, like the fire of hell, at last: "O Mother Earth, who art no more my Mother, and into whose bosom this frame shall never be resolved! O mankind, whose brotherhood I have cast off, and trampled thy great heart beneath my feet! O stars of heaven, that shone on me of old, as if to light me onward and upward! —farewell all, and forever. Come, deadly element of Fire, —henceforth my familiar friend!" (III, 496) And even Aylmer hears the mocking laughter of his own "familiar," the "earth-fiend" Aminadab, as his high attempt to correct nature succeeds—and is paid for by the death of his beautiful wife. Hawthorne's work is, in fact, replete with personages who appear to have made a bargain with infernal agencies in exchange for knowledge or power—wizards like the one in "Alice Doane's Appeal" and like Matthew Maule in *The House of the Seven Gables,* as well as the necromancers and alchemists who are Hawthorne's "scientists." It is no accident that Hawthorne's scientists are not scientists at all in the nineteenth-century sense, but occultists of various sorts. Hawthorne's allegories represent them as men who have bargained illicitly for the gifts of mind. Perhaps most explicit, though a minor example of the Faust compact in Hawthorne's fiction, is the bargain made by the scholarly pastor, George Burroughs, in "Main Street." "In the very strength of his high and searching intellect," Hawthorne says of him, "the Tempter found the weakness which betrayed him. He yearned for knowledge; he went groping onward into a world of mystery . . . he summoned up the ghosts of his two dead wives . . . and, when their responses failed to satisfy the intense and sinful craving of his spirit, he called on Satan, and was heard" (III, 469-70).

Stewart has observed that Hawthorne's villains are all "incarnated devils"—Chillingworth, for example, is derived from the devils and wizards of the early tales.[8] One feels that his peculiar gifts are acquired by the Devil's aid. This may help to account for the lack of satisfactory characterization in Hawthorne's villains. They are not really human, after all. The mental energy they seem to possess is the Devil's gift. When Chillingworth has finished his work and his victim is dead, he is snatched to the Devil's bosom and all his demoniacally inspired force vanishes in a moment, as though the terms of a pact were now exacted.

> All his strength and energy—all his vital and intellectual force—seemed at once to desert him; insomuch that he positively withered up, shrivelled away, and almost vanished from mortal sight, like an uprooted weed that lies wilting in the sun. This unhappy man had made the very principle of his life to consist in the pursuit and systematic exercise of revenge; and when, by its completest triumph and consummation, that evil principle was left with no further material to support it, when, in short, there was no more Devil's work on earth for him to do, it only remained for the unhumanized mortal to betake himself whither his Master would find him tasks enough, and pay him his wages duly (V, 307).

The evil Westervelt is seen as another soul possessed, if not as the Thief of Souls himself. Like the Devil, in "Young Goodman Brown" he appears suddenly in the forest twilight, even bearing an identical staff carved with the likeness of a snake. When he laughs, Coverdale catches sight of the gold band of his false teeth and is oddly affected:

> I felt as if the whole man were a moral and physical humbug; his wonderful beauty of face, for aught I knew, might be removable like a mask; and tall and comely as his figure looked, he was perhaps but a wizened little elf, gray and decrepit, with nothing genuine about him, save the wicked

expression of his grin. The fantasy of his spectral character so wrought upon me, together with the contagion of his strange mirth on my sympathies, that I soon began to laugh as loudly as himself (V, 427-28).

The particular faculty of Chillingworth and Westervelt —as of Dr. Rappaccini, perhaps, and the wizard Maule—is one peculiarly akin to the artist's, as already remarked; they possess that piercing eye which enables them to see into ordinary men. Two other characters gain this same power by real or symbolic compacts with the Devil. It will be recalled that Young Goodman Brown finds himself suddenly empowered with the terrible ability to see the evil truth in all men after he has partaken of the Devil's sacrament in the forest. And Dimmesdale, walking homeward from his interview with Hester beside the forest brook, which has seemed to gain him a release from conscience, suddenly sees evil hidden in the bosom of each person whom he meets and asks himself: "Am I mad? or am I given over utterly to the fiend? Did I make a contract with him in the forest, and sign it with my blood?" (V, 263)

Similarly Faustian, as we shall see, are Hawthorne's artists. Oberon, the narrator of "The Devil in Manuscript," speaks of "that conception in which I endeavored to embody the character of a fiend, as represented in our traditions and the written records of witchcraft . . . a hellish thing [who] used to suck away the happiness of those who, by a simple concession that seemed almost innocent, subjected themselves to his power." "Just so," he tells his friend, "my peace is gone, and all by these accursed manuscripts. Have you felt nothing of the same influence?" To which the narrator replies, "Nothing, unless the spell be hid in a desire to turn novelist, after reading your delightful tales."

> "Novelist!" exclaimed Oberon, half seriously. "Then indeed, my devil has his claw on you! You are gone! You cannot even pray for deliverance!" (III, 575)

The artist who paints the foreboding portraits in "The Prophetic Pictures" is a close relation to the characters discussed above. Reading "other bosoms with an acuteness almost preternatural, the painter failed to see the disorder of his own" (I, 207). "Are you telling me of a painter or a wizard?" asks Elinor (I, 192). The common people considered him to be "a magician, or perhaps the famous Black Man, of old witch times, plotting mischief in a new guise," but "even in superior circles his character was invested with a vague awe, partly rising like smoke wreaths from the popular superstitions, but chiefly caused by the varied knowledge and talents which he made subservient to his profession" (I, 195). When the tragedy of Walter and Elinor reaches its foreordained climax and the insane husband aims his knife at his wife's bosom, the artist-magician is seen again.

> He had advanced from the door, and interposed himself between the wretched beings, with the same sense of power to regulate their destiny as to alter a scene upon the canvas. He stood like a magician, controlling the phantoms which he had evoked (II, 209).

Hawthorne, of course, does not imply that Coverdale or Kenyon or Holgrave or Owen Warland, or any other of his artists, is a Gothic villain, but they all seem to have gained their powers by the sacrifice of some essential element of heart, and we often get the feeling that an idealized version of the Faustian compact forbids them love and heaven so long as they accept the Devil's help. It would seem to be no accident that Holgrave is a descendant of the wizard Matthew Maule, whose mesmeric powers he inherits, together with the family trait of solitariness. When Holgrave does achieve human happiness and spiritual salvation in his marriage to Phoebe, one gathers that it is because, unlike Marlowe's Faustus, he cried "I'll burn my books!" in time.

More important, however, than the criticism supplied by pessimistic Romanticism was the argumentative recourse that Hawthorne found in the Puritan tradition. However much he qualified the religious dogmas of his ancestors, Hawthorne, as I have already remarked, was supremely conscious of the relevance of the ethical viewpoint they had transmitted to him—the traditional Christian viewpoint, with its censure of pride as the master sin, its conviction that man is a compound of evil and good, its insistence upon the moral measure of all things. He applied this critique to the artist, as to other men; particularly to the artist, however, as I have suggested, because Romantic theory seemed bent on endowing the creative individual with a special status of immunity, a privilege of self-expression and amoralism which was intolerable to the Christian creed.

There was more seriousness than jest in Hawthorne's speculation (in the introduction to *The Scarlet Letter*) as to what his "stern and black-browed" Puritan ancestors would have thought of an idler like himself:

> No aim that I have ever cherished, would they recognize as laudable; no success of mine—if my life, beyond its domestic scope, had ever been brightened by success—would they deem otherwise than worthless, if not positively disgraceful. "What is he?" murmurs one gray shadow of my forefathers to the other. "A writer of story-books! What kind of a business in life,—what mode of glorifying God, or being serviceable to mankind in his day or generation,—may that be? (V, 25)

In the same mood, half-mocking, half-serious, the first lay occupant of the Old Manse considered the lesson proposed for him by surroundings steeped in the traditions of generations of Protestant sermon writers:

> I took shame to myself for having been so long a writer of

idle stories, and ventured to hope that wisdom would descend upon me with the falling leaves of the avenue, and that I should light upon an intellectual treasure in the Old Manse well worth those hoards of long-hidden gold which people seek for in moss-grown houses. Profound treatises of morality; a layman's unprofessional and therefore unprejudiced views of religion; histories (such as Bancroft might have written had he taken up his abode there as he once purposed) bright with picture, gleaming over a depth of philosophic thought, —these were the works that might fitly have flowed from such a retirement. In the humblest event I resolved at least to achieve a novel that should evolve some deep lesson and should possess physical substance enough to stand alone (II, 12-13).

Hawthorne was troubledly aware of the Puritan judgment of the arts, but this does not mean that he considered the attitude of the seventeenth century narrowly moralistic, or opposed to the free display of artistic effects. As Kenneth Murdock has pointed out, the "ancient heresy" that the Puritan was "hostile" to art as such needs rectification for many modern persons, but it did not for Hawthorne. He knew that the Puritan had not condemned all artistic creation, but "other things in life came first. . . . To satisfy a pious colonist a book must work; it must teach, console or record what should not be forgotten."[9] Such an attitude was not the same as the philistine doctrine of utility, or the moralistic gentility which took the place of morals for Hawthorne's contemporaries. Hawthorne's view of art also was moral, but not moralistic—despite his objection to nude statuary. From a sense of the relation of personal behavior to the general well-being, he seems to have believed that the artist was obliged to find a social function, to achieve communicability, to preach wisdom. Otherwise he had no right to waste the wits which industry might put to more fruitful human employment.

We will notice that Hawthorne frequently brings the Puritan frame of reference into his stories about artists or artist types. Nor does he scorn to invoke the superstitions, stemming from the age in which the Devil was a real personage who might meet one behind every door, for these, too, provide the atmosphere of a moral universe which the Puritan recognized. Hawthorne resolved to find in *The House of the Seven Gables* the human nature buried in the ancient superstitions with which his story dealt. This is probably his aim wherever he makes use of such traditional prejudice. So, in "The Gentle Boy," where the Puritan moral judgment, together with primitive superstition, condemns the excesses of Catherine the Quakeress, he seems to ask whether there is not a fundamental truth in their censure, and whether her "Romantic" excesses are not the manifestations of a soul "possessed" by evil impulses. In "The Prophetic Pictures," he asks us to consider seriously what human truth may lie in the suspicion that the artist was a sort of wizard, perhaps the Black Man of the forest.

The Magic Work of Art

Hawthorne, as we have seen, was wont to speak loosely of the "magical" properties of a work of art. We have seen the roots of this commonplace idea in transcendental aesthetics: if the artist is an inspired miracle-worker, then his productions are magic objects. The artist is a practitioner of *white magic,* which owes its strength to the master magician, God. In imitating God's creation, the artist molds "living" works out of dead materials. On the other hand, as I have suggested, Gothic tradition provided the alternative theory of a sort of *black magic* practiced by a Faustian necromancer-artist. His works also have "living" qualities which enable them to work harm upon human beings. We shall presently see that in "The Artist of the Beautiful"

Hawthorne demonstrates that a true work of art has an organic wholeness rivaling that of a living organism, and that, if the artist has breathed his soul into it fully, it can truly be said to "live," as Owen Warland's mechanical butterfly can be said to have acquired the quality of life through its creator's inspiration. The Gothic portraits painted by the artist of "The Prophetic Pictures" represent a grotesque parody of this idea. They are also "alive," but after the fashion of Melmoth's portrait with the blazing eyes. The transcendental view of art here displays its demonic opposite; the white magic of the seer-poet becomes the black magic of the wizard.

The products of such artistic magic abound in Hawthorne's writings. The painting which plays the role of a supernatural agency is seen not only in "The Prophetic Pictures," but in "Edward Randolph's Portrait," in *The House of the Seven Gables* (where the daguerreotype is also a part of the symbolic structure), and in the tale "Sylph Etherege." The statue which comes alive is used not only in the story of the woodcarver Drowne, but in "The Snow Image," and, in a sense, in "Feathertop." *The Marble Faun* is a perfect side show of magic works of art.

Sometimes these are examples of the holy creativeness of the artist; sometimes they are agencies of his evil tendencies. Almost always they tell us something about Hawthorne's view of the artist. Even when the creator of the work of art is not a part of the story—as, for example, in the case of the Malbone miniature in *The House of the Seven Gables*—it is impossible to regard these magic objects as conventional fictional devices, like the manuscript hidden in the wall. They were a profoundly attractive type of symbol to Hawthorne precisely because his mind dwelt constantly on the enigma of the power of art, and constantly asked the question: Is it a good power or an evil one? The ambiguity of these symbols represents Hawthorne's division of mind.

As Eino Railo has shown, the magic work of art is one of the standard furnishings of the haunted Gothic castle:

> Ever since the portrait of Hamlet's father and that of Ricardo saw the light, pictures of long-departed friends or relatives have in general played an important role in romantic stories. In the heated brains of the romanticists, the old conception of a picture awakening to life which happens when Walpole makes Ricardo's picture step out of its frame gradually acquired new substance and with the passage of time accumulated new details. . . . In Mrs. Radcliffe's works it becomes a miniature invested with tender memories; it displays in every castle hall the features of ancestors; and finally proves effectual in transmitting a sombre impression of that mysterious wanderer on the face of the earth, Melmoth. From the very beginnings of terror-romanticism it exercised a special fascination on authors; it is to them not merely an inanimate object, but in some enigmatical way an animated being, like the picture in *The Castle of Otranto*.[10]

In the stories written by some of the greatest nineteenth-century writers the theme transcends its horror-tale aspects and reaches expressive importance. Examples are Poe's story "The Oval Portrait," Hoffman's "Doge and Dogaressa," and Gogol's "The Mysterious Portrait." Poe's story can be taken as an example of how these artists made use of the Gothic theme. Setting out to explain the origin of a "living" art-work, he tells the story of an artist who paints the portrait of his beloved, but in his absorption fails to observe that his model is pining slowly away, her life passing into his masterpiece.

> He passionate, studious, austere, and having already a bride in his art; she a maiden of rarest beauty, and no more lovely than full of glee; all light and smiles and frolicsome as the young faun; loving and cherishing all things, hating only the art which was her rival; dreading only the palette and

brushes and other untoward instruments which deprived her of the countenance of her lover.[11]

Poe, like Hawthorne, is concerned with the dangerous egotism of the artist. In "The Oval Portrait," the artist's pursuit of the ideal of art has resulted in the death of the human element, or, more precisely, the human element has been absorbed into art and has perished there.

We can recognize this story pattern in "The Birthmark," a tale which does not involve the creation of a work of art. As Aylmer labors to achieve the materialization of ideal beauty in his wife, he loses sight of her as a human being, and, achieving his end, finds that he has taken her life. Exactly the same theme was used by Balzac in his long tale "The Quest of the Absolute," which tells of the tragic success of a scientist who attains the secret of the philosopher's stone but ruins his family, causes the death of his wife, and utterly destroys his bonds with mankind. So the moral of Hawthorne's "The Prophetic Pictures" is that the artist's power is a potential curse. The story would seem to relate that it was merely the truth-telling, prophetic faculty of the painter in the tale which gave such sinister significance to the portraits he painted of Walter and Elinor Ludlow. Actually, more is implied. We are shown the character of the artist himself. He is a man of great perceptive gifts, but of cold emotions. His relation to life is the relation of the portraits to the sitters—the relation of impersonal study to its object. And such a relation damages because it excludes affection. So art itself, the portraits themselves, are instruments of harm—they can reveal the future, they can warn, but they cannot assist.

"Edward Randolph's Portrait," the second of the four "Legends of the Province House," in *Twice-Told Tales,* contains a true Gothic portrait which is reminiscent of the mysterious portrait with the staring eyes in *The Bride of*

Lammermoor. Its demonic character is suggested early in the story by Captain Lincoln, who relates to Alice Vane some of "the fables and fantasies which, as it was impossible to refute them by ocular demonstration, had grown to be articles of popular belief, in reference to this old picture" (I, 295). Hawthorne, despite his urbane disparagement of superstition, always means us to take such "fables and fantasies" seriously. As I shall show in the similar case of "The Prophetic Pictures," he invokes Puritan prejudice to suggest Puritan faith, and surrounds his narrative by this means not merely with an atmosphere of quaintness but of seventeenth-century moral judgment. Thus: "One of the wildest, and at the same time the best accredited, accounts, stated it to be an original and authentic portrait of the Evil One, taken at a witch meeting near Salem; then its strong and terrible resemblance had been confirmed by several of the confessing wizards and witches, at their trial, in open court" (I, 295). The painting is not merely occult, but, one feels certain, demonic.

It turns out to be a portrait, not of the Devil, but of one of his servants, Edward Randolph, who is supposed to be suffering eternal damnation for having trampled on the rights of the people. The painting is revealed, from beneath the dark obscurity which had covered it for years, through the earnest patriotism and artistic skill of Alice Vane, seeking to warn her uncle, Governor Hutchinson, of the danger of flouting the popular wish. She "restores" the picture— that is, makes it a "living" art-work, able to act upon the beholder with a power not granted to mere inanimate cloth and paint. Artist-magician that she is, the gentle Alice cleans the old canvas and cries to it, "Come forth, dark and evil Shape! . . . It is thine hour" (I, 299). Thus she reveals the terrible fate of the Governor's predecessor, and warns the present administrator of the province that the same fate waits for him. Like the artist of "The Prophetic Pictures," she warns in vain.

The possible genesis of the tale may be interesting to note here, for it strengthens our impression that in this story Hawthorne was interested in the theme of the power of art and was not merely employing the magic-portrait device as a bit of Gothic machinery. Robert Cantwell suggests that Hawthorne wrote it as a forecast of the fate of the class of wealthy Cuban colonials, after reading the journal Sophia had kept during her stay at one of the island's great estates. As a matter of fact, the problem confronting families like the de Zayas was much like that which challenged Hutchinson; they were torn between their love for the old country and their sense of being exploited by it. On August 2, 1834, Sophia recorded in her diary that she had spoiled her portrait of the young Don Fernando de Zayas: "It was the most beautiful soul-beaming face I have ever produced— but a touch of the pencil is omnipotent and a false one banished the living soul from the features and changed his noble look into an expression of utter stupidity and ordinariness." "Hawthorne," says Cantwell, "plainly meant to imply that her mistake was the reality."[12] He saw in Sophia the gift of prophetic force.

The statue that comes to life is another common Gothic device,[13] with a more ancient prototype in the classical story of Pygmalion. Hawthorne, who retold the old Greek myths with such charm, took the tale of Pygmalion and transferred it to Colonial New England in "Drowne's Wooden Image." But this is the story of a piece of white magic; Hawthorne has been less Gothic than transcendental in this parable of the power of love to animate the creations of artistic ingenuity. The modest woodcarver, whose productions have been only clever figureheads and gateposts, one day fashions a statue that arouses the admiration of Copley. "Here is the divine, the life-giving touch," he cries. And the artist explains that while he labored upon this female figure "a wellspring of inward wisdom gushed within me as I wrought upon the oak with my whole strength, and soul, and faith"

(II, 353, 355). Love has given genius to the Yankee wood-carver. *His* achievement has been the reverse of egotistical; indeed he makes no claim for what has been accomplished through his hands. "Can it have been my work? Well, I have wrought it in a kind of dream; and now that I am broad awake I must set about finishing yonder figure of Admiral Vernon" (II, 361).

The duality in Hawthorne's view of the artist is neatly displayed by the symbolism of two stories. In "The Prophetic Pictures," art is shown to be an instrument of evil, the egotistical fruit of cold curiosity. In "Drowne's Wooden Image" we are told that the true work of genius is inspired by love and reverence for its subject. Curiously, the demonic, "black magical" aspects of art are nearly always represented by painting, while sculpture tends to symbolize the living works of Romantic genius that are divine in origin. The statue that comes alive through love, at which we have just glanced in "Drowne's Wooden Image," appears in several slighter versions in Hawthorne's tales. Hawthorne subtitles his story "The Snow Image" "A Childish Miracle," for it is a story about, and possibly for, children, written in the tender, musing bedtime tone of the father of Una and Julian. Yet the theme of two children who make a snow-child in front of their home one winter morning was also of interest, one suspects, to the mature artist who never tired of reflecting upon the nature of his calling.

The story actually parallels "Drowne's Wooden Image" very closely. As the children work at their image, says the author, "it seemed, in fact, not so much to be made by the children, as to grow up under their hands, while they were playing and prattling about it" (III, 394). No more than Drowne, then, could they account for what they suddenly found themselves able to accomplish. And indeed, comments Hawthorne, "if miracles are ever to be wrought it will be by putting our hands to the work in precisely such a simple and undoubting frame of mind as that in which Violet and Peony now undertook to perform one, without so much as knowing that it was a miracle" (III, 393). The life-giving breath of love is communicated to the image, just as Drowne the sculptor wrought his masterpiece under love's influence. The children even kiss its frozen lips— "Perhaps, Peony, it will make them red if we both kiss them!" (III, 399). And sure enough, the miracle comes to pass, and the little snow-girl dances in the frozen garden with her playmates.

But a miracle must be believed to make itself felt, and, if it is a work of art we are talking about, a creative master-piece must come alive in the heart of each appreciator. The children's mother was fit audience for their achievement. Her character "had a strain of poetry in it, a trait of un-worldly beauty,—a delicate and dewy flower, as it were, that had survived out of her imaginative youth . . . (III, 391). As she watches her boy and girl at work—"Peony bringing fresh snow, and Violet applying it to the figure as scientifi-cally as a sculptor adds clay to his model" (III, 397)—she is both amused and tender. She smiles to see "how their little imaginations had got mixed up with what they were doing, and carried away by it. They seemed positively to think that the snow-child would run about and play with them" (III, 398). "They make me almost as much a child as they themselves are!" she muses as she watches them. "I can hardly help believing, now, that the snow-image has really come to life!" (III, 400). Of course, it is honest Papa, who reminds one of Peter Hovenden in "The Artist of the Beautiful," who insists that snow is snow and flesh is flesh and that if this is a little girl without a coat on she must be made to sit down by the fire and wait till her white cheeks are thawed. His pragmatic viewpoint destroys the snow-maiden as surely as Peter's materialism destroys Owen's butterfly.

And here we may remark upon the curious quality of the central symbol in "The Artist of the Beautiful," the animated mechanical butterfly which, though it must represent all the arts, is neither painting nor sculpture, but a scientific toy. As shall be seen when the story is examined in detail, Owen's marvelous piece of handiwork is an organic achievement, a miracle of artistic creation which rivals nature. It is an authentic Romantic symbol of the work of art. And yet, being a mechanism which duplicates only an insect's soulless beauty it cannot represent human love for the human as can either Drowne's image of a beautiful woman or the snow-child. The butterfly, as we shall see, is the work of idealism, but not of human love. It is an embrace of love, on the other hand, that Copley glimpses Drowne bestowing upon his ship's figurehead and a kiss that the children give to their white playmate. Perhaps even the witch's broomstick-turned-man, in the story "Feathertop," is such an animated statue, a sort of Pinocchio, who, if he had won Polly Gookin, might have turned into a real boy. As Feathertop himself says, "methinks a kiss from her sweet lips might have made me altogether human" (II, 277). And *The Marble Faun,* one remembers, was titled *Transformation* when published in England, for its whimsical motif is the conversion of the Faun of Praxiteles into a man at the hands of his three artist friends, when his relation to them becomes one of human sympathy. The "living" statue is one of Hawthorne's favorite symbols for the work of art that has achieved vital being because human affection has gone into its making.

The House of the Seven Gables and *The Marble Faun* are full of works of art which represent the penetrative and predictive function of the artist. The first contains at least three magical portraits: the miniature of Clifford by Malbone, which Hepzibah cherishes as a portrait of her brother in his youthful beauty; the painting of Colonel Pyncheon which hangs in the Pyncheon mansion; and the daguerreotype which Holgrave has taken of the living Judge Pyncheon. Of these, the second, the most conspicuously Gothic, is probably the least interesting. Colonel Pyncheon's portrait is directly out of the Gothic tradition—the fatal family portrait of Clara Reeves' *The Old English Baron,* the walking portrait of *The Castle of Otranto;* it fails to express anything more, probably, than ancestral doom. More symbolically interesting, if less important in the plot of the novel, are the other two.

When Phoebe finally beholds the shattered Clifford, she recognizes the original of Hepzibah's cherished miniature. This had displayed "a likeness of a young man, in a silken dressing-gown of old-fashion, the soft richness of which is well adapted to the countenance of reverie, with its full tender lips, and beautiful eyes, that seem to indicate not so much capacity of thought, as gentle and voluptuous emotion (III, 48), Now, however,

> . . . he seemed to sit, with a dim veil of decay and ruin betwixt him and the world, but through which, at flitting intervals, might be caught the same expression, so refined, so softly imaginative, which Malbone—venturing a happy touch, with suspended breath—had imparted to the miniature! There had been something so innately characteristic in this look, that all the dusky years, and the burden of unfit calamity which had fallen upon him, did not suffice utterly to destroy it (III, 132).

This, too, is a prophetic picture, for Clifford, with his sensitive aesthetic nature, was to prove unfit to cope with the tragedy that was dealt him. His gentle and voluptuous sensibility is all that remains to him after the long duress of his unjust imprisonment.[13] Yet Malbone has not predicted the ruin of Clifford so much as the essential virtue and grace in the personality of the sitter, the portion of his nature that was to survive disaster.

In the story "Sylph Etherege" Hawthorne seems to sug-

gest that there may be a peril in an idealizing art, a peril as
pernicious in its way as the bitter truth of the prophetic
portraits. In this tale the unprepossessing Edgar Vaugham
comes to claim the bride to whom he has been betrothed
since childhood, but who has never seen him, and, posing
as a friend of the fiancé, shows her an exquisite ivory miniature which her soul immediately identifies as a portrait of
her lover. But when he reveals his cruel deception to Sylph,
Vaughan finds that he cannot win back her love from the
phantom he has conjured up. The dream is more real than
the fact. In anguish he exclaims, "Can our sweet Sylph be
going to heaven, to seek the original of the miniature?"
(III, 517) Here, again, the work of art has been magical,
for it has created a reality powerful enough both to compel
love and cause death.

Holgrave's daguerreotype of Judge Pyncheon is an extremely interesting representation of Hawthorne's ideas
about an up-to-date, truth-telling art—the method of realism, which is yet "magical" because it is art, and does
therefore disclose what is hidden to the common gaze. One
cannot help thinking of that extraordinary daguerreotype
of Hawthorne himself which was taken in 1848,[14] and wondering how it impressed the subject of the exquisite Osgood
portrait, which has been reproduced so many more times.
This daguerreotype shows a lean, hard face, a scowling
mouth, an unsparing, brilliant glance; the head is turned
toward the camera in an attitude of unwilling pause. Here
is a Hawthorne the Peabodys seldom saw—the son of a sea
captain who died of fever in far-off Surinam. That it was
nevertheless truth-telling is indicated by a remarkable pen-
portrait by Samuel Goodrich, which matches it as if the
writer had had the picture itself before him.[15]

Holgrave's daguerreotype portrait of Judge Pyncheon
shows the hidden identity of the living Pyncheon with the
colonial ancestor whose doom has descended to him. Just as

Judge Pyncheon is a reincarnation of the first Pyncheon, he shall inherit the curse of the wizard Maule. Phoebe thinks for a moment that the subject of Holgrave's picture is the same man who posed for the painting of her ancestor hanging in the parlor of the House of the Seven Gables. The daguerreotype has revealed the true malevolence and craft beneath the smiling exterior which Judge Pyncheon presents to the world. Says Holgrave:

> There is a wonderful insight in Heaven's broad and simple sunshine. While we give it credit only for depicting the merest surface, it actually brings out the secret character with a truth no painter would ever venture upon . . . yet the original wears, to the world's eye,—and, for aught I know, to his most intimate friends,—an exceedingly pleasant countenance, indicative of benevolence, openness of heart, sunny good-humor, and other praiseworthy qualities of that cast. The sun, as you see, tells quite another story, and will not be coaxed out of it, after half a dozen patient attempts on my part (III, 116-17).

When Phoebe is confronted by the Judge himself, she recognizes the original of the daguerreotype, and asks herself:

> Was it, therefore, no momentary mood, but, however skillfully concealed, the settled temper of his life? And not merely so, but was it hereditary in him, and transmitted down, as a precious heirloom, from that bearded ancestor, in whose picture both the expression, and, to a singular degree, the features of the modern Judge were shown as by a kind of prophecy? (III, 146-47)

So, in symbolic fashion, the daguerreotype represents the Maule curse transferred by the artist's insight (and by a lineal descendant of the wizard Maule) onto the smiling face of Judge Pyncheon.

In *The Marble Faun* Hawthorne's initial whimsy was

the "transformation" of the Faun of Praxiteles into a living man, by the addition of love and conscience. This change is also represented in the book by the history of another sculptured work, the bust of Donatello which Kenyon makes during his visit to the villa of the Counts of Monte Beni. The history of this portrait-bust will be discussed in connection with the character of its creator, the artist Kenyon, in a later chapter. Let us note here, however, that Kenyon's work is still another magic statue. Wrought *through* rather than *by* the sculptor, it represents his intuitive knowledge of past and future, for during its successive stages of modeling it exhibits Donatello's crime and his future expiation of it, by the expressions momently fixed in the clay under his hands.

The artist's prophetic, divinatory function is viewed in both its good and its evil potential through the magic works of art that throng *The Marble Faun.* In Miriam's studio Donatello finds sketches that predict her savage revenge upon her persecutor, and even a lay figure accidentally posed in a posture of desperate appeal such as she will soon make to him in person. Hilda, though only a copyist, has produced a remarkable duplication of Guido's portrait of Beatrice Cenci, and it is discovered by her friends that she herself has come to resemble it, in its embodiment of innocence stained by unwilling participation in evil, after she has witnessed the crime of Donatello and Miriam. Still another prophetic work of art is the sketch of the archangel Michael vanquishing the demon, also by Guido, which Miriam and her friends happen upon at a party; it is discovered that Miriam's persecutor has been strikingly anticipated by Guido's painting of the demon.

The curious reader may, indeed, identify other strangely animated works of art in the novel, for the characters of *The Marble Faun* seem never to leave for long the question of art and its power to harm and help. That the life of art is a principal theme of *The Marble Faun* these numerous symbolic and occult objects indicate clearly enough—indeed, the book is so studded with references to works of art, "living" and dead, that one tends to ignore all of the aesthetic material in the book as mere ballast for the abstract moral argument upon which most criticism has concentrated. Actually, I believe, the theme of art is Hawthorne's major one; it is no accident that three of the four chief characters are artists, and that the questions of their moral destiny and of the nature of their art are closely intermingled in the novel. Miriam, we shall later see, is another example of the fated, devil-haunted "prophetic painter." Hilda soon discovers that her vocation is not for the morally perilous life of art, but for sympathetic copying of the work of others. And Kenyon, who embraces the love of Hilda in the end, will soon, we feel, renounce the tragic vision which had enabled him to create his bust of Donatello. In this fable of art and life the characters are accompanied, we shall find, by works of art embued with celestial or satanic vitality, constant symbolic reminders, as such objects always are in Hawthorne's fiction, of art's power to bless or to damn.

NOTES TO CHAPTER III

1 Canto III, Stanza 59.

2 See Jane Lundblad, *Nathaniel Hawthorne and the Tradition of Gothic Romance* (Cambridge, Mass.: Harvard University Press, 1947) ; and Neal Frank Doubleday, "Hawthorne's Use of Three Gothic Patterns," *College English*, VII (1946) , 250-62.

3 *Shelburne Essays, First Series*, pp. 69-70.

4 *American Notebooks*, p. lxxxv.

5 *Ibid.*, p. 117.

6 See Eino Railo, *The Haunted Castle: A Study of the Elements of*

English Romanticism (London: G. Routledge and Sons, 1927), pp. 191-218.

[7] William Bysshe Stein, in *Hawthorne's Faust: A Study of the Devil Archetype* (Gainesville, Fla.: University of Florida, 1953), has noted the numerous references to devils and demonic pacts which bestrew Hawthorne's stories and novels, and has concluded that they represent the central "archetype" of his fiction. The significance of this omnipresent motif he states as follows: "Symbolically the ritual act of commitment is implemented whenever a character in his stories, either in thought or deed, endorses a mode of conduct that violates the conventional code or infringes upon natural human rights. To indicate that an illicit state of affairs prevails, Hawthorne ordinarily invokes the mythic image of the devil" (p. 51). In his search for devils and devil-compacts which symbolize man's involvement with general Evil, Stein tends to obscure the more specific meaning of the Faust story as a warning against intellectual aspiration and pride, and to read inaccurately the meaning of those stories in which this more restricted meaning becomes paramount. In subsequent pages I shall refer to my particular disagreement with Stein's analysis of "The Artist of the Beautiful" and "Drowne's Wooden Image."

[8] *American Notebooks,* p. liii.

[9] "The Puritan Tradition," in Foerster, *Reinterpretation of American Literature,* pp. 105-6.

[10] Railo, *The Haunted Castle,* pp. 54, 305.

[11] *Complete Poems and Stories of Edgar Allan Poe,* ed. Arthur Hobson Quinn and Edward H. O'Neill (New York: Alfred A. Knopf, 1946), I, 383.

[12] *Nathaniel Hawthorne: The American Years* (New York: Rinehart, 1948), pp. 233-56.

[13] Malbone's work was apparently famous for this discernment. Tuckerman relates that a foreign artist once recognized in the miniature by Malbone of a beautiful girl of seventeen, the features of an old lady to whom he had recently been introduced. Henry J. Tuckerman, *Book of the Artists: American Artist Life* (New York: G. P. Putnam and Sons, 1867), p. 122.

[14] Reproduced in *The Proceedings in Commemoration of the One Hundredth Anniversary of the Birth of Nathaniel Hawthorne* (Salem, Mass.: The Essex Institute, 1904), p. 13. A reproduction of this daguerreotype is also shown on the dust-jacket of the present book, through courtesy of The Essex Institute.

[15] ". . . his hair dark and bushy, his eye steel gray, his brow thick, his

mouth sarcastic, his whole aspect cold, moody, distrustful. . . . At this period he was unsettled in his views; he had tried his hand in literature and considered himself to have met with a fatal rebuff from the reading world" (Samuel Goodrich, *Recollections of a Lifetime, or Men and Things I Have Seen* [New York and Auburn: Miller, Orton and Mulligan, 1856], II, 270) .

Chapter IV

The Artist of the Beautiful

~~~~~~

A contemporay British reviewer observed in Tait's *Edinburgh Magazine* that if Emerson had written a short story, he would have written "The Artist of the Beautiful."[1] It is true that the tale seems to be composed in the intellectual language of Romantic transcendentalism. The key polarities of Reason and Understanding, Heart and Head, Imagination and Fancy, are put to work in an allegory which represents Hawthorne's most sympathetic treatment of the idealistic view of artistic creation. Here, if anywhere in his fiction, we see the part of Hawthorne's speculation represented by the remarks assembled in Chapter II, his passive assent to the transcendental exaltation of art and the artist. Yet it does not seem to me that the story can be termed, as it has been by Richard H. Fogle, "a Romantic apologia for the artist, which concludes by affirming his moral superiority to all other conceivable categories of humanity."[2] Read carefully—and it must be read carefully, for it is an extremely subtle and intricate little work—"The Artist of the Beautiful" is a piece of delicate irony in which the story that might have been told by Emerson is given its fullest chance, and gently put aside for proving its case too well.

Thus we are shown, indeed, that the artist is able to create an image of the beauty inaccessible to other men—but *not* that he thereby brings that beauty into their lives, as Emerson and the English Romantics would have added. Rather, the artist is deemed incapable of communicating the eternal truths apprehended in his lonely ecstasies. One gets the impression that somehow Hawthorne has split the Romantic design which gave the poet-seer his special *mission* among men. Hawthorne has, in this story, pushed idealism so far that it becomes a criticism of itself. As demonstrated in the parable of Owen Warland, the realm of the true and the beautiful is forever removed from the world of actuality, and Nature is not the poet's teacher, but his antagonist. Life gives no aid to the artist and cannot be affected by his discoveries, for his work itself is but a paltry visible demonstration of the inexpressible splendor within him.

Art is not a social activity, consequently. Not only is it irrelevant, it may even be inimical to the normal human pattern of love and happiness. The Imagination, the faculty of Reason and the Heart, seems, indeed, capable of producing the antihuman effects of the Understanding, the faculty of the Head. Hawthorne's artist is one of those "persons whose pursuits are insulated from the common business of life—who are either in advance of mankind or apart from it"—apparently it makes no difference which—and who experience "a sensation of moral cold that makes the spirit shiver as if it had reached the frozen solitudes around the pole" (II, 518). The effect of this "Defence of Poesy" is damning. Finally, Hawthorne does not even say that art is tragic, only that it is pathetic, like a summer butterfly crushed in a child's hand.

One can imagine Hawthorne writing this story in the Manse, surrounded by Sophia's gold-colored wallpaper and transcendental enthusiasm, looking up now and then to see Emerson or Thoreau or Ellery Channing or Margaret Ful-

ler come into view, and being very much in love with the
whole happy atmosphere, willing to give it fairest play. So
he undertakes to tell with utter tenderness the story of
Owen Warland, the frail, unloved young watchmaker who
fashions a mechanical butterfly so exquisite that it cannot
be told from a real one. Owen, unlike Aylmer in "The
Birthmark," succeeds in his search for the Beautiful, but
only because he acknowledges before it is too late that the
actual and the ideal cannot be brought together without
fatal consequences. He rejects all of life which comprises
its warm reality, even casts off at last his art-work itself for
being less ideal than the vision in his soul. One may well
wonder whether Hawthorne, full-alive, in love, and yet
determined to be an artist, approved this ultimate consequence of the transcendental aesthetic.

The tensions of the plot are drawn between familiar
opposites, as we have said. Fundamental, of course, is the
antithesis between matter and spirit. Tiny, frail, sensitive
Owen is the representative of the spirit, with least of fleshly
substance. In contrast with him, the blacksmith Robert
Danforth, his rival for Annie Hovenden, is sturdy materiality. Hawthorne repeatedly makes the point that size and
physical force have no relation to spiritual importance.
Owen is small in body, and his mind, we are told, is "microscopic, and tended naturally to the minute" (II, 507). But,
observes Hawthorne, "The beautiful idea has no relation
to size and may be as perfectly developed in a space too
minute for any but microscopic investigation as within the
ample verge that is measured by the arc of the rainbow"
(II, 507-8). In the perfect beauty of the miraculous butterfly which Owen fashions, "the consideration of size was
entirely lost. Had its wings overreached the firmament the
mind could not have been more filled or satisfied" (II, 530).
When Danforth boasts to the artist, "I put more main
strength into one blow of my sledge hammer than all that

you have expended since you were a 'prentice," Owen answers, "Very probably. . . . Strength is an earthy monster. I make no pretensions to it. My force, whatever there may be of it, is altogether spiritual" (II, 510). He laughs at the idea that he may be trying to discover the secret of perpetual motion—*such* a search is "a dream that may delude men whose brains are mystified with matter, but not me" (II, 510).

His aim is more closely guessed at by chattering young Annie, as she hands him her thimble to be fixed: "But I don't know whether you will condescend to such a task, now that you are so taken up with the notion of putting spirit into machinery" (II, 517). He himself confesses when he thinks of her: ". . . if I strive to put the very spirit of beauty into form and give it motion, it is for thy sake alone" (II, 509). But Annie is no more capable than the blacksmith of understanding Owen's object. He, in turn, is oblivious of the earthy, material Annie, seeing only the ideal which he worships in her image: ". . . she was the visible shape in which the spiritual power that he worshipped, and on whose altar he hoped to lay a not unworthy offering, was made manifest to him" (II, 523). It was she in whom he hoped to find "a finer grace which might enable her to be the interpreter between strength and beauty" (II, 527).

Matter's most formidable champion is Annie's father, old Peter Hovenden, whose materialistic skepticism, embodied in his tiny grandson, finally destroys the symbolic butterfly. " 'Let us see,' said Peter Hovenden, rising from his chair, with a sneer upon his face that always made people doubt, as he himself did, in everything but a material existence. 'Here is my finger for it to alight upon. I shall understand it better when once I have touched it' " (II, 533).

But with the flight of the butterfly from its maker's hands, Owen's idealism has reached its highest level. He no longer expects to spiritualize matter; he no longer needs Annie to interpret between strength and beauty. Like the boy pictured on the carved gift-box in which he has presented the wedding gift to Annie, he has transcended matter altogether.

> It was carved richly out of ebony by his own hand, and inlaid with a fanciful tracery of pearl, representing a boy in pursuit of a butterfly, which, elsewhere, had become a winged spirit and was flying heavenward; while the boy, or youth, had found such efficacy in his strong desire that he ascended from earth to cloud, and from cloud to celestial atmosphere, to win the beautiful (II, 529).

The material embodiment of the ideal is no longer itself important, "symbolizing a lofty moral by a material trifle" (II, 532). After the butterfly has been destroyed by "the little child of strength," Owen is described as looking

> placidly at what seemed the ruin of his life's labor, and which was yet not ruin. He had caught a far other butterfly than this. When the artist rose high enough to achieve the beautiful, the symbol by which he made it perceptible to mortal senses became of little value in his eyes while his spirit possessed itself in the enjoyment of the reality (II, 535-36).

It is spirit, then, that is the true reality, and not matter. With this final statement should be contrasted the praise which the materialist Hovenden earlier accorded the blacksmith: "He spends his labor upon a reality." The butterfly Owen creates is a "real" butterfly; it is alive, Owen tells Annie, because it has absorbed the soul of the artist.

The basic spirit-matter antithesis is underscored in the story by several secondary pairs of contrasting ideas. Eternity, the boundless scale of the spiritual realm, is set against clock time, which records duration in the material world. Hawthorne thoroughly enjoys ringing all the possible changes on the symbolism provided by the watchmaker's trade. Hovenden, in denouncing Warland's ingenuity as a threat to the health of the timepieces entrusted to him, declares: "He would turn the sun out of its orbit and derange the whole course of time" (II, 505). Again: "He altogether forgot or despised the grand object of a watchmaker's business, and cared no more for the measurement of time than if it had been merged into eternity" (II, 508). The townspeople soon realized "how unfit a person was Owen Warland to lead old blind Father Time along his daily course" (II, 508). One of Owen's projects was a system by which the machinery of his watches was connected with a musical device, "so that all the harsh dissonances of life might be rendered tuneful, and each flitting moment fall into the abyss of the past in golden drops of harmony" (II, 508). The soberer citizens of the town shook their heads over this and kindred freaks, and the young watchmaker soon lost credit "with that steady and matter-of-fact class of people who hold the opinion that time is not to be trifled with" (II, 509). Following the destruction of his first attempt to create the symbol of the Beautiful, Owen becomes an exemplary watchmaker, and it is the opinion of Peter Hovenden and "that order of sagacious understandings who think that life should be regulated, like clockwork, with leaden weights" (II, 512), that the alteration has been for the better. Owen now respects earthly Greenwich time and regulates the clock in the church steeple, so that the "town in general thanked Owen for the punctuality of dinner time" (II, 513). And even Peter Hovenden becomes more genial and offers to let Owen work on his precious old watch, which he values almost as much as he does his daughter Annie. Owen demurs, but Hovenden says, "In time . . . in time, you will be capable of it" (II, 514).

As spirit is opposed to matter, and eternity to clock time, beauty is opposed to practicality. Owen the artist, with his

impractical vision of the Beautiful, is contrasted with
Hovenden and the blacksmith. Since childhood, Owen has
been "remarkable for a delicate ingenuity... always for
purposes of grace, and never with any mockery of the useful" (II, 507). Hence, he cannot successfully harness his
skill to the practical ends of the watchmaker's trade. Hovenden scorns Owen's ability with the remark, "All the effect
that ever I knew of it was to spoil the accuracy of some of
the best watches in my shop" (II, 505). Even when he has
succeeded in his object and wrought his butterfly as an
image of ideal beauty, the blunt Robert Danforth can only
exclaim: "That goes beyond me, I confess. But what then?
There is more real use in one downright blow of my sledge
hammer than in all the five years labor that our friend
Owen has wasted on this butterfly" (II, 532). Only when
Owen's artist-soul is in a temporary eclipse, and he gives up
his dream of the Beautiful, is he able to win the respect of
his fellow townsmen as a reliable watchmaker, repairing
the town clock to everyone's wholehearted satisfaction.

These polar opposites of spirit and matter, eternity and
time, beauty and practicality, have their obvious corollaries
in the faculties of the mind. Thus, Hawthorne identifies
Owen the artist with the higher Reason or the Imagination
—as Kant, or Coleridge, or Emerson would have defined it
—and exemplifies the Understanding in Peter Hovenden
and his daughter, Robert Danforth, and the town's other
sober citizens. Although Owen hoped to imbue matter with
spirit, or to find in Annie a human mediator between the
two realms, we see that he ends by acknowledging that no
reconciliation is possible between the invisible Truth that
he has reached and the limited truths visible to his fellow
men. By means of the Imagination, the artist aspires to
knowledge of the pure forms, the Platonic absolutes, which,
according to transcendental philosophy, Nature is constantly in the process of approximating. It was Owen's aim

to produce "a beauty that should attain to the ideal which Nature has proposed to herself in all her creatures, but has never taken pains to realize" (II, 524). It is his Imagination that enables the artist to reach this higher truth—invisible, eternal, nonpractical—whereas such a man as Peter Hovenden is able to employ only the base faculty of Understanding. Peter Hovenden possessed, writes Hawthorne, that "keen understanding ... which saw so distinctly what it did see, and disbelieved so uncompromisingly in what it could not see" (II, 521-22). None prove capable of apprehending the artist's vision. The townspeople judge him to be mad, as such as they have always judged the seer.

> How universally efficacious—how satisfactory, too, and soothing to the injured sensibility of narrowness and dullness— is this easy method of accounting for whatever lies beyond the world's most ordinary scope. From St. Paul's days down to our poor little Artist of the Beautiful, the same talisman had been applied to the elucidation of all mysteries in the words of men who spoke or acted too wisely or too well (II, 521).

Not even the intuitive perceptions of the Woman and the Child, those two allies of the Romantic artist, confirm the discoveries of Hawthorne's lonely Artist of the Beautiful. In a moment of illusion, Owen dreamed that Annie Hovenden, with her more delicate and sympathetic nature, could share his vision, and so indeed she might have, the author comments, "had she been enlightened by the deep intelligence of love" (II, 519). Annie's infant son, far from recognizing the butterfly as a messenger from his recent abode in the realm of Spirit, behaves as one would expect a young child to do; he smashes the new toy in his strong little hands.

Owen's struggle is seen as a conflict between the Imagination and the "mind-forged manacles" of the Understanding.

When Annie's marriage to Danforth blights the artist's spirit and causes him to surrender his pursuit of the Beautiful for awhile, he becomes a temporary champion of the Understanding. He loses "his faith in the invisible," prides himself "in the wisdom which rejected much that even his eye could see, and trusted confidently in nothing but what his hand could touch" (II, 525). Hovenden, as the chief representative of the Understanding, declares himself unable to understand the miraculous butterfly until he has actually touched it with his finger. For Owen, this viewpoint is "the calamity of men whose spiritual part dies out of them and leaves the grosser understanding to assimilate them more and more to the things of which alone it can take cognizance" (II, 525).

The artist's creation, defined in the same scheme that includes the transcendental definitions of reality and of the mental faculties, is, unlike the work of the mere Fancy, an organism that rivals the living creatures of God's making. It is no longer just a mechanism. "Is it alive?" asks Annie. And Owen answers: "Alive? Yes, Annie; it may well be said to possess life, for it has absorbed my own being into itself; and in the secret of that butterfly, and in its beauty,—which is not merely outward, but deep as its whole system,—is represented the intellect, the imagination, the sensibility, the soul of an Artist of the Beautiful!" (II, 531). Robert Danforth in his crude way expresses the matter by exclaiming, "Well, that does beat all nature!" (II, 532). That the butterfly is an organism rather than a clockwork mechanism makes it not only, of course, a true work of art, but a symbol of the universe conceived romantically. The watch, on the other hand, is the favorite eighteenth-century metaphor for a universe which is a logical system of parts. Plainly, Peter Hovenden the watchmaker lives mentally in the pre-Romantic cosmos; Owen's world is alive, interfused with "a motion and a spirit that impels/All thinking things, all objects of all thought,/And rolls through all things." Likewise, the beauty of the butterfly is organic—"not merely outward but deep as its whole system" (II, 531). As a work of art it resembles the Romantic universe. It has organic form, which is, as Coleridge said, "innate; it shapes as it develops itself from within, and the fulness of its development is one and the same with the perfection of its outward form."[3]

Now that we have laid out the chief philosophic stress-lines in "The Artist of the Beautiful," it remains to be considered whether the system as a whole really works exclusively in the direction they indicate. My opinion is that it does not. The story, as I have suggested, is more subtly organized, so as to produce effects of irony that continually subject the philosophic pattern to a curious sort of vibration between belief and disbelief.

As the tale opens, we encounter Hovenden and his daughter in the process of contemplating first Owen Warland and then the blacksmith. With them, we glance quickly into Owen's shop window to see the watchmaker stooped over his finicking work, and then we behold his rival standing at the forge. Owen, we soon are told, is conscious of possessing "a finer, more ethereal power, of which this earthly giant can have no conception" (II, 511). But Hawthorne's descriptive imagination has been playing curious tricks on us meanwhile. For, as Annie and her father pass the blacksmith's shop, we are permitted a sight extraordinarily compelling:

Within was seen the forge, now blazing up and illuminating the high and dusky roof, and now confining its lustre to a narrow precinct of the coal-strewn floor, according as the breath of the bellows was puffed forth or again inhaled into its vast leathern lungs. In the intervals of brightness it was easy to distinguish objects in remote corners of the shop and the horseshoes that hung upon the wall; in the momentary gloom the fire seemed to be glimmering amidst the vagueness of unenclosed space. Moving about in this red glare and alternate dusk was the figure of the blacksmith, well worthy to be viewed in so picturesque an aspect of light and shade, where the bright blaze struggled with the black night, as if each would have snatched his comely strength from the other. Anon he drew a white-hot bar of iron from the coals, laid it on the anvil, uplifted his arm of might, and was soon enveloped in the myriads of sparks which the strokes of his hammer scattered into the surrounding gloom (II, 505-6).

At no point in the story will we ever get a picture of Owen Warland that can contend with this. Remembering this figure, we will smile, half-consciously, to read that when the agitated Owen accidentally destroyed his tiny piece of work, his look of horror "made his small features as impressive as those of a giant would have been" (II, 511). The contrast of brute matter with spirit is insistently displayed to us as the contrast of "comely strength" with weakness. It has already been mentioned that Hawthorne stresses the smallness of Owen's body and the microscopic scale of his mind, which loved to express itself in work of gossamer substance. The effect of this information—putatively—is, as I have indicated, to make Owen a symbol of the spiritual. But as an image, this association of tinyness is restricting— think, in this connection, of the contrary connotations carried by words developed from concepts of size, such as "grandeur," "loftiness," or "magnitude" (importance). Despite the fact that Hawthorne warns us that "the beautiful idea has no relation to size," the anguish of little Owen over his "little whirligig," as Annie calls it, stirs us much less than it should. One has merely to consider what Swift accomplished by manipulating our conventional reaction to size to realize how powerfully we tend to "belittle" what is physically diminutive.

The limiting effect of symbols is felt in Hawthorne's choice for the image of the Beautiful—a butterfly. As we have noted, Owen's creation is organic and alive, a marvel of delicate beauty, and "had its wings overreached the firmament, the mind could not have been more filled or satisfied." But the very assertiveness of Hawthorne's statement raises a suspicion that Hawthorne does not quite expect our reactions to go this way. Indeed, in his earliest novel, *Fanshawe,* he had used the same image quite differently. Of the life of the tavern poet Hugh Crombie, Hawthorne wrote: "The winter, therefore, was his season of prosperity; in which respect he differed from the butterflies and useless insects, to which he otherwise bore a resemblance" (XI, 113). How light and *unimportant* this representation makes the activity of the idealist Owen! Throughout the story one receives the impression that the choice of allegorical representation accomplishes a deliberate adjustment of the theme. One feels the results of a considerable humor working behind the exalted tone of the ideas presented, which inclines one to suspect that Hawthorne felt, like Annie, "a secret scorn—too secret, perhaps, for her own consciousness" (II, 532), for the artist. It cannot be denied, certainly, that the artist's destiny, as represented by the figure of Owen Warland, appears not so much tragic and important as merely pathetic.

How convincing, on the other hand, is the opposition provided by Owen Warland's antagonists, old Hovenden, Annie, and the blacksmith Robert Danforth. Of the three, Hovenden alone seems to match with personality and attitude the materialism that is attributed to him. Danforth's sturdy integrity, seen always in the light of the forge of human purpose or by the hearth of the domestic affections, is, as we have seen, actually attractive. He is no earth fiend Aminadab when Owen finds him in his domestic beatitude, "the man of iron, with his massive substance thoroughly

warmed and attempered by domestic influences" (II, 527).
Annie Hovenden—whose relatives in Hawthorne's fiction
are Phoebe Pyncheon in *The House of the Seven Gables,*
Rose Garfield in *Septimius Felton,* Dorothy Pearson in
"The Gentle Boy," Ellen Langton in *Fanshawe,* and Susan
in "The Village Uncle"—is actually of a type of feminine
charm very close to Hawthorne's ideal. We picture her as
being like these other engaging, natural, affectionate, but
unintellectual women of the Heart.

Owen's triumph, with which the story ends, takes place
at the hearth of the married pair Danforth and Annie,
where, with something of the same persuasive strength seen
in the early description of the blacksmith at the forge, the
superior wholeness of their happiness is communicated by
the scene itself, whatever contrary superscription Hawthorne writes upon it. A curious reciprocating irony works
back and forth in this scene. Let us examine, for example,
Hawthorne's description of the child, which Owen sees for
the first time:

> The artist did not immediately reply, being startled by the
> apparition of a young child of strength that was tumbling
> about on the carpet,—a little personage who had come mys-
> teriously out of the infinite, but with something so sturdy and
> real in his composition that he seemed moulded out of the
> densest substance which earth could supply (II, 528).

Here is the Child, whose claim to supernal connection is as
good as the Artist's. Yet he is sturdy and real, made out of
"the densest substance which earth could supply," and it
is he who actually destroys the butterfly. Though we are
told that the child has something of his grandfather's shrewd
expression, we do not completely identify him with old
Hovenden. Instead, the infant seems to represent normal
human possibility, the human complex of matter and spirit,

compared to which the purely spiritual symbol of art is but a plaything.

Let us now look in a slightly different fashion than before at the thesis which the story proposes—that the artist is the unique representative of the spiritual aspect of life. As I have suggested, Hawthorne has expressed through his allegory an idealism so intense that one may be justified in wondering if he is not trying to discover the logical outcome of ideas he does not entirely trust. To begin with, the very abstractness of his artist's goal—for the transcendental "Beautiful" divorced from any meaning recognizable in life or nature—tends to make it seem less moving and important. We shall presently contrast with Owen the painter of "The Prophetic Pictures," whose art—portraiture—does concern itself with life and is tragically involved with human fates. "In truth, it was seldom his impulse to copy natural scenery, except as a framework for the delineations of the human form and face, instinct with thought, passion, or suffering" (I, 205). *This* artist, whom one cannot help believing to have been a closer representation of Hawthorne the novelist, stirs our sympathy more profoundly. Owen's ideal aim keeps his art from doing harm—and keeps it unconnected with the human experience.

We are told that Owen Warland succeeded in his effort to create an image of the Beautiful. Yet we see at once that here is no Carlylean "hero as poet," for Owen is unable to communicate his discoveries to those around him. Hawthorne concludes that the idealist artist will be misunderstood and unappreciated:

Thus it is that ideas, which grow up within the imagination and appear so lovely to it and of a value beyond whatever men call valuable, are exposed to be shattered and annihilated by contact with the practical. It is requisite for the ideal artist to possess a force of character that seems hardly compatible with its delicacy; he must keep his faith in himself while the incredulous world assails him with its utter disbelief; he must stand up against mankind and be his own sole disciple, both as respects his genius and the objects to which it is directed (II, 512).

In this passage, as Austin Warren has observed,[4] we seem to hear Hawthorne speaking out of his own experience. Melville triple-scored it,[5] and it is easy to suppose why. Like Hawthorne, he was acutely aware of the *penalties* of being an artist—suspicious, perhaps, of the easy raptures of the transcendentalist, who assumed that the poet was the prince of the human commonwealth. Certainly his is not a conclusion Emerson would have approved. Or we can compare it with the well-known passage in the Preface to the *Lyrical Ballads,* in which Wordsworth expresses his belief that the true poet is the harmonizer of society.[6]

Owen's "triumph," like Georgiana's dying praise of Aylmer in "The Birthmark," seems but half-comfort for his surrender of human happiness. All of Hawthorne's other studies of the artist will show us how he viewed isolation and divorce from the brotherhood of affection as the price of a too exclusive attention to abstract ends. Like any Faust,[7] Owen is tempted by a love which is forbidden him. He cannot say, "Stay, thou art so fair!" when he listens to the bright chatter of Annie Hovenden come into his shop to have her thimble fixed. "Owen Warland's story would have been no tolerable representation of the troubled life of those who strive to create the beautiful, if, amid all other thwarting influences, love had not interposed to steal the cunning from his hand" (II, 522). Hawthorne's tone seems as much sardonic as it is tender. He observes that if Owen had succeeded in winning Annie and she had proved to be what his artist's soul imagined, "his lot would have been so rich in beauty that out of its mere redundancy he might have wrought the beautiful into many a worthier type than he had toiled for" (II, 523). It is not clear just what our writer means here. In view of the later parallels of Holgrave and Kenyon—artists who surrender their service to art for the warmer beauty of human love—one suspects that the "worthier type" of the Beautiful was to be wrought not in the medium of art, but of life. On the other hand, if successful love had brought Owen to the realization that Annie was less than he had dreamed, "the disappointment might have driven him back, with concentrated energy, upon his sole remaining object" (II, 523). So the creation of the Beautiful seems to be contingent upon the severing of the artist from normal channels of happiness.

In the light of this conclusion we must ask what has become of the terms "Head" and "Heart," which seem to play a role in the story together with the complimentary pairs, Understanding and Reason, Fancy and Imagination. Hawthorne's frequent use of the contrast between Head and Heart has been widely noted.[8] But it has not been stressed sufficiently that he uses the terms ambiguously rather than in accordance with the transcendental definition. The artist, above all other men, is supposed to be the exponent of Heart. He is gifted with intuitive kinship with the deepest feeling—as Winckelmann said, *"der Geist und das Gefühl mehr als Kopf."* In "The Artist of the Beautiful," Owen Warland seems at first to be the spokesman of Heart, and the watchmaker, his daughter, and the blacksmith to be exponents of the "meddling intellect." Yet Owen's fate indicates that he has chosen to sever himself from the forge and the hearth—twin symbols of the warmth of society—and to pursue the isolate aims of the Head. He is like Aylmer, we shall see, in placing a nonhuman object above the dictates of the affections. He is—and we shall press the analogy even thus far—like Dr. Rappaccini, who as he contemplates the results of his mental labors, gazed at his vic-

tims "as might an artist who should spend his life in achieving a picture or a group of statuary and finally be satisfied
with his success" (II, 146). He is, in other words, at once
seer and creator, *and* the upstart who rivals Nature by the
exercise of false wit. The result, says Hawthorne, is "moral
cold."

> To persons whose pursuits are insulated from the common
> business of life—who are either in advance of mankind or
> apart from it—there often comes a sensation of moral cold
> that makes the spirit shiver as if it had reached the frozen
> solitudes around the pole (II, 518).

The same will be said of the painter of "The Prophetic
Pictures."

Finally, it is well to consider what Hawthorne's allegory
does to the work of art itself. The idealism that is represented by "The Artist of the Beautiful" is so extreme that
it places between the material and the spiritual realms a
barrier that is absolute. Not only is the artist and his spiritual experience divorced from common experience, but the
materialization of his ideal, the tangible product of his
dreams, is inferior to his immaterial vision. This, we have
seen, is standard Romantic principle, subscribed to elsewhere by Hawthorne. But in this story he sees the pathos
rather than the glory of such a view.

> Alas that the artist, whether in poetry, or whatever other ma-
> terial, may not content himself with the inward enjoyment
> of the beautiful, but must chase the flitting mystery beyond
> the verge of his ethereal domain and crush its frail being in
> seizing it with a material grasp (II, 516).

The artist must reconcile himself to the fact that his work
will always be incomplete.

The poet leaves his song half sung, or finishes it, beyond the scope of mortal ears, in a celestial choir. The painter—as Allston did—leaves half his conception on the canvas to sadden us with its imperfect beauty, and goes to picture forth the whole if it be no irreverence to say so, in the hues of heaven. But rather such incomplete designs of this life will be perfected nowhere. This so frequent abortion of man's dearest projects must be taken as a proof that the deeds of earth, however etherealized by piety or genius, are without value, except as exercises and manifestations of the spirit. In heaven, all ordinary thought is higher and more melodious than Milton's song. Then, would he add another verse to any strain that he had left unfinished here? (II, 526-27)

Owen was therefore indifferent to the fate of the actual butterfly he had made with his ingenious watchmaker's fingers. "He had caught a far other butterfly than this" (II, 535).

But it is, after all, a melancholy triumph.

NOTES TO CHAPTER IV

1 January, 1855, citeα in Bertha Faust, *Hawthorne's Contemporaneous Reputation* (Philadelphia: University of Pennsylvania, 1939), p. 112.

2 "The World and the Artist: A Study of Hawthorne's 'Artist of the Beautiful,'" *Tulane Studies in English,* I (1949), 32. This essay, the most important study to date of "The Artist of the Beautiful," appears in revised form in *Hawthorne's Fiction: the Light and the Dark* (Norman, Okla.: University of Oklahoma Press, 1952), where the phrase quoted by me is omitted, though Fogle continues to call the story "a Romantic affirmation of the value of art and of the spiritual pre-eminence of the artist's imagination, which intuitively penetrates to highest Goodness, Truth, and Beauty" (p. 78). Fogle has noted the

Romantic polarities which are discussed here, concluding from their presence that "in 'The Artist of the Beautiful' Hawthorne expounds the fundamental ethic, metaphysic, psychology, and aesthetic of English Romanticism" (p. 76). But, as I shall show, Hawthorne proposes, *only to reject*, the Romantic exaltation of the artist, which is based upon the assumed superiority of the Imagination over other faculties, and of the higher claims of ideality, eternity, and beauty. Moreover—as Fogle fails to observe—Hawthorne actually reverses the traditional roles of "head" and "heart," perhaps the most significant antithesis of all, identifying his artist *not* with the heart, which is the moral twin of the imagination in Romantic ethics, but with the head, which is the partner of the earth-bound understanding. Unlike previous analyses, Fogle's sensitive reading takes into consideration the imaginative *testing* of themes which Hawthorne practices. He "furnishes material for other interpretations than his own," Fogle says. "His characters may and should be read allegorically both as types and ideas, but they become complex human beings as well, creatures of mingled strength and weakness, good and evil" (p. 81). After conceding some of the ambiguities which Hawthorne's imaginative process creates, he concludes: "Hawthorne's intention clearly is to present Owen Warland as the spiritual norm of his tale and to proclaim through him the superior significance and intensity and the greater value of the artist's experience and interpretation of reality . . . however, Warland does not always show up well in his environment. This fact is a tribute to Hawthorne's imaginative honesty. The artist is in some degree Hawthorne himself, and therefore it is all the more necessary that he avoid manipulating the fictional truth in his favor. So, as is his custom, Hawthorne leans backward—at times a little too far backward" (p. 86). But it seems to me that in his readiness to discover in Hawthorne "the light and the dark" (simplicity of design complicated by ambiguity) Fogle fails to recognize that Hawthorne does resolve his paradox of the artist—by viewing him as an alien, albeit a harmless one, at the warm hearth of human values, making no contribution there, for all his exalted connection with the supernal. And this judgment—essentially a stern one—is finally made, I believe, without equivocation. It is more certainly Hawthorne's own view of the artist.

[3] *Coleridge's Shakespearean Criticism,* ed. T. M. Raysor (Cambridge, Mass.: Harvard University Press, 1930), I, 224.

[4] *Nathaniel Hawthorne: Representative Selections* (New York: American Book Co., 1934), p. 366.

[5] Matthiessen, *American Renaissance,* p. 223.

6 "In spite of all difference of soil and climate, of language and manners, of laws and customs, in spite of things silently gone out of mind, and things violently destroyed, the poet binds together by passion and knowledge the vast empire of human society, as it is spread over the whole earth, and over all time."

7 Owen Warland is indeed one of Hawthorne's Fausts, but his symbolic bargain and its consequences have been radically misinterpreted by William Bysshe Stein in *Hawthorne's Faust*. Stein notes that Owen declares to Peter Hovenden: "You are my evil spirit . . . you and the hard coarse world!" and he concludes that Owen is being tempted from his salvation by "materialism." Writes Stein of the artist's eclipse before his final self-conquest: "The devil's gifts, which obscure the values of the spirit, are not easily rejected, for at last even the baffled youth surrenders his dreams to the mercenary god" (pp. 94-95). But certainly Owen is never tempted by "mercenary" gifts. Indeed, he is a Faust in quite an opposite sense—in having bargained for the occult powers of the mind, the artist's creative magic, and paid the price of dehumanization. He is not "saved" in the end, as Stein implies, but "damned" for being unable to love. "In the symbolic overtones of this tale [Hawthorne's] criticism of rampant materialism and spiritual starvation rings out with unrelenting harshness," Stein concludes, but the story's contemporaneity is of quite another kind, as I have shown; its "Devil" is more likely what the Romantics called the Spirit of the Absolute.

8 See Warren, *Nathaniel Hawthorne*, pp. xlv-xlvii; Matthiessen, *American Renaissance*, p. 345; and Donald A. Ringe, "Hawthorne's Psychology of the Head and Heart," *PMLA*, LXV (1950), 120-32.

Chapter V

Two Colonial Artists

~~~~~~

The Painter of the "Prophetic Pictures"

If "The Artist of the Beautiful" is a melancholy defense of the life of art, "The Prophetic Pictures" touches the tragic center of Hawthorne's view of the evil inherent in the artist's occupation. Written some years before the story of Owen Warland, "The Prophetic Pictures" belongs to the period before Hawthorne's marriage, when he was most personally concerned with the isolating, perverting effects of his role as a writer.[1] In construction, it is far simpler than the later story. Theme and allegory are combined with the directness of a folk parable, uncomplicated by the subtle equivocations of the tale of Owen Warland. Yet "The Prophetic Pictures" loses nothing by comparison with its companion-piece. It is, indeed, an example of Hawthorne's poetic imagination working on possibly a deeper level. It is uncluttered by the dictum and aphorism which provide the somewhat artificial structure of ideas in "The Artist of the Beautiful," and it compasses a wider range of emotions. Narrative and characterization contain its entire statement.

The germ of the tale was an incident related by the American art historian William Dunlap concerning Gilbert Stuart:

Lord Mulgrave employed Stuart to paint the portrait of his brother, General Phipps, previous to his going abroad. On seeing the picture, which he did not do until it was finished, Mulgrave exclaimed, "What is this?—this is very strange!" and stood gazing at the portrait. "I have painted your brother as I saw him," said the artist. "I see insanity in that face," was the brother's reply. The general went to India, and the first account his brother had of him was that of suicide from insanity. He went mad and cut his own throat. It is thus that the real portrait-painter dives into the recesses of his sitters' minds.[2]

Hawthorne acknowledges his indebtedness to Dunlap for the germ of his story, calling his source "a most entertaining book to the general reader, and a deeply interesting one, we should think, to the artist" (I, 192), but proceeds to shift the elements of the incident until they serve his purpose.

To Dunlap the story plainly was an illustration of the penetrative faculty of the artist, an instance of his superiority over ordinary persons. This view of the artist's power is expressed in the story itself, for Hawthorne has Walter Ludlow, one of the subjects of the fatally prophetic pictures, declare:

They say he paints not merely a man's features, but his mind and heart. He catches the secret sentiments and passions, and throws them upon the canvas, like sunshine—or perhaps, in the portraits of dark-souled men, like a gleam of infernal fire (I, 193).

But Hawthorne's chief interest is not this. As Newton Arvin observes:

What interested him was not so much the sitters and their tragedy as the artist and his: for him the artist's power was always a potential and here an actual curse; his art might so easily become "an engrossing purpose" which would "insu-

late him from the mass of humankind," as this painter's does,
and transform him indeed from the mere reader of men's
souls into an agent of their destinies.[3]

Consequently, Hawthorne changes completely the atmosphere and the personages presented in the original anec-
dote. The action takes place in a more remote past (Stuart
had died less than ten years before Hawthorne wrote "The
Prophetic Pictures"), a little later than the earliest colonial
period. The unnamed artist of the tale antedates even the
first native painters. He was "not one of those native artists
who, at a later period than this, borrowed their colors from
the Indians, and manufactured their pencils from the furs
of wild beasts" (I, 194), but an educated Englishman, prac-
ticing his sophisticated art in provincial Boston, and in the
tiny settlements that were like merest sparks against the
black of the continental wilderness. The reader familiar
with Hawthorne will recognize this background—that of
The Scarlet Letter, "The Maypole of Merrymount,"
"Young Goodman Brown," "The Gentle Boy," and the
sketches of colonial life—in which Christian ethic and
superstition combine to pass judgment upon the passions
of the human upstart, and the primeval forests remind him
of his demonic heart. By setting the story back into this
earlier historical moment, Hawthorne places the problem
of art within the moral critique of the Puritans. His artist,
with his detached relation to life, his restless wandering,
his nostalgia for wild nature, is a figure out of the nineteenth century, judged by the standards of the seventeenth.
Hawthorne discarded altogether the characters of his
source-story. He changed Stuart's sitter, the historic General
Phipps, into a couple—Walter Ludlow and his bride Elinor
—for whom the artist's brush forecasts a fatal interaction:
he to grow to madness and murder, she to sorrow and terror.
The familiar and tangible Stuart, moreover, becomes a

nameless and haunting figure, introverted and restless—rather Byronic, perhaps. At the same time, he is clothed in a threatening mystery. The common people half believe him to be a magician, or the famous Black Man of the forest: "Even in superior circles his character was invested with a vague awe, partly rising like smoke wreaths from the popular superstitions, but chiefly caused by the varied knowledge and talents which he made subservient to his profession" (I, 195). As always, Hawthorne's ironic deprecation is a blind for the moral energy which emanates from his use of Puritan creed and prejudice. He means nothing to be taken more seriously than precisely these "smoke wreaths" which reach even our twentieth-century nostrils with vaguely troubling odors of guilt and hell-fire.[4]

Hawthorne has reshaped the story, moreover, so as to establish a dramatic relation between the painter and the subjects of his portraits. Stuart's disclosure of the character of Phipps does not establish any further connection between them. It was Hawthorne's point, however, that the artist is responsible to the human beings he comes to know so intimately; he cannot assume that their fates are only subjects for the display of his mental keenness, unless he aims to comfort and heal. The painter, after he has achieved his prophetic representation of the secret selves of the young couple, declares, like Stuart in the story of Mulgrave's brother, "I have painted what I saw," but he tells this to his subjects themselves. "If I have failed," he tells Elinor—"if your heart does not see itself reflected in your own portrait—if you have no secret cause to trust my delineation of the other—it is not yet too late to alter them. I might change the action of these figures, too. But would it influence the event?" (I, 202-3). And he directs her attention to a sketch in which not merely the character development of the portraits is visible, but the combining action which will give meaning to the expressions on the faces—Walter in the act of stabbing the terrified Elinor. But the pictures are painted and in due time hang in the parlor of the newly married pair, though after awhile Elinor puts a silken curtain in front of them under the pretense that dust or sunlight may affect their hues. Friends familiar with the pictures discern a growing resemblance between the master and mistress of the house and their portraits—a look of wildness flashing across Walter's face, a mournfulness falling over Elinor's.

Meanwhile, the painter traverses the wild forests of New England, filling his portfolio, as Hawthorne was wont to fill his notebooks during his wanderings through the same region, "with graphic illustrations of the volume of his memory, which genius would transmute into its own substance and imbue with immortality" (I, 205). The recollection of his portraits of Walter and Elinor accompanies him on his way, but it is not anxiety or tenderness that holds their images before him.

> So much of himself—of his imagination and all other powers —had been lavished on the study of Walter and Elinor, that he almost regarded them as creations of his own, like the thousands with which he had peopled the realms of Picture. Therefore did they flit through the twilight of the woods, hover on the mist of waterfalls, look forth from the mirror of the lake, nor melt away in the noontide sun. They haunted his pictorial fancy, not as mockeries of life, nor pale goblins of the dead, but in the guise of portraits, each with the unalterable expression which his magic had evoked from the caverns of the soul. He could not recross the Atlantic till he had again beheld the originals of those airy pictures (I, 206).

He does indeed return to see them, and to see his prediction fulfilled. "Wretched lady!" he says to Elinor as he steps between her and her crazed husband, "did I not warn you?" "You did," she answers. "But—I loved him!" (I, 209)

In other words, mere knowledge is powerless to avert disaster. Hawthorne concludes the story with the moral:

> Could the result of one, or all our deeds, be shadowed forth and set before us, some would call it Fate, and hurry onwards, others be swept along by their passionate desires, and none be turned aside by the PROPHETIC PICTURES (I, 210).

What exactly does this mean? That prophetic knowledge will not save the doomed man any more than knowledge of his doom saved Oedipus? The story as a whole says more. *Knowledge without pity* is inhuman and will not turn men from the destiny toward which their own natures carry them pell-mell; it is useless in the moral scheme.

The painter of "The Prophetic Pictures" should be set beside the watchmaker-artist Owen Warland for a complete view of Hawthorne's concept of the artist. Seeming at first diametric opposites, upon examination they are discovered to be different views of the same personality. No less than the Artist of the Beautiful, the prescient portraitist is the dedicated Romantic idealist, continually striving for a beauty which lies beyond the mundane sphere, indifferent to the common purposes of men. "He had no aim—no pleasure—no sympathies—but what were ultimately connected with his art" (I, 206). His hymn to art is as exalted in tone as Owen's salutation might have been:

> O glorious Art! . . . thou art the image of the Creator's own. The innumerable forms, that wander in nothingness, start into being at thy beck. The dead live again. Thou recallest them to their old scenes, and givest their gray shadows the lustre of a better life, at once earthly and immortal. Thou snatchest back the fleeting moments of History. With thee there is no Past, for, at thy touch, all that is great becomes forever present; and illustrious men live through long ages, in the visible performance of the very deeds which made them what they are. O potent Art! As thou bringest the

faintly revealed Past to stand in that narrow strip of sunlight, which we call Now, canst thou summon the shrouded Future to meet her here? Have I not achieved it? Am I not thy Prophet? (I, 207)

The passage begins, it should be noted, with an invocation to Art as the image of the Creator's own activity, and ends with an announcement of the artist's prophetic function. Coleridge declared that imagination was the creative faculty which resembled the divine power, "a repetition in the finite mind of the eternal act of creation in the infinite I AM."[5] To Emerson, likewise, human art was merely another expression of the divine art which informs the natural world. It is in this sense that the artist is to be regarded as godlike, or at least as a seer, a prophet. In the artistic act he creates, sees, and foretells.[6] Now we need not, of course, take Hawthorne's "prophetic" transcendentally. Yet the association of Poet and Prophet was a current intellectual shibboleth ringing in his ears as he wrote his story of a painter whose work literally did foretell the future. Hawthorne seems to be examining the intellectual result of the deification of the artist which he must have observed in the writings of the German and English transcendentalists, and in Emerson's.

Consider, for example, the doctrine of aesthetic irony, which he may or may not have heard about, but which follows logically from the apotheosis of the artist. The English and American Romantics were, of course, little affected by this German amoralism, which was the fad of Schlegel, Tieck, and Novalis rather than of Wordsworth, Coleridge, or Carlyle. As Fairchild puts it, "If the English romanticist is a priest of art, he remains a parish priest with a cure of souls."[7] But the German writers may have been significant for the Americans who were just then trying to read them, grammar and dictionary in hand. At any rate, the attitude of Hawthorne's painter-prophet provides us with a perfect example of aesthetic irony. As the Germans decreed, he was sovereign of his created universe as God is of His, remote, paring his nails.[8] And this was a posture Hawthorne strongly condemned. Yet looking back we see that Owen Warland of "The Artist of the Beautiful" was as indifferent to the human scale of emotion as the ironic painter, and as susceptible of this condemnation, though he harmed no one with his transcendental pursuit of the Beautiful.

What Hawthorne is at pains to show in the story is the menace of those very qualities upon which the Romantic artist prided himself. The naïve Walter, as we have already mentioned, is impressed by the painter's gift of catching the secret light of his sitters' souls. But he adds, "I shall be almost afraid to sit to him" (I, 193). After the painter agrees to undertake the portraits of Walter and Elinor, the young man asks his sweetheart with a smile if she is aware of the influence over their fates that the painter is now about to acquire.

> "The old women of Boston affirm," continued he, "that after he has once got possession of a person's face and figure, he may paint him in any act or situation whatever—and the picture will be prophetic. Do you believe it?"
>
> "Not quite," said Elinor, smiling. "Yet if he has such magic, there is something so gentle in his manner that I am sure he will use it well" (I, 198).

Despite Elinor's trust, we feel that the instinctive fear of the narrow-minded populace may have a certain validity—as did the educated members of the colonial community, as a matter of fact.

> Some deemed it an offence against the Mosaic law, and even a presumptuous mockery of the Creator, to bring into existence such lively images of his creatures. Others, frightened at

the art which could raise phantoms at will, and keep the form of the dead among the living, were inclined to consider the painter as a magician, or perhaps the famous Black Man, of old witch times, plotting mischief in a new guise. These foolish fancies were more than half believed among the mob. Even in superior circles his character was invested with a vague awe, partly rising like smoke wreaths from the popular superstitions, but chiefly caused by the varied knowledge and talents which he made subservient to his profession (I, 195).

As I have suggested before, these doctrinal and superstitious criticisms represent Hawthorne's own serious fears, by way of symbolizing them. Though his nineteenth-century mind did not accept the primitive terms of these beliefs, it could utilize them as a mythic representation of the traditional Christian judgment which still maintained its validity for him. By this device, the painter's Romantic amoralism is confronted by the Puritan standard of humility and duty.

We have spoken earlier of the Gothic art-work as a device which Hawthorne found repeatedly useful not only as a sensational effect but because it might suggest the "living" qualities of art and its power for good and evil. The double portrait of Walter and Elinor is such a work. The Gothicism is so subtle and Hawthorne's apparently realistic handling of his story so accomplished that we almost miss the sleight-of-hand by which the atmosphere of black magic, diabolism, infernal witchery, and the rest is let down over the painter. Hawthorne begins, for example, by telling us quite straightforwardly that Walter and Elinor, like most people, were charmed with the idea of an imperishable representation of themselves, and in a characteristic passage, he remarks:

Nothing in the whole circle of human vanities, takes stronger hold the imagination than this affair of having a portrait painted. Yet why should it be so? The looking-glass, the polished globes of the andirons, the mirror-like water, and all other reflecting surfaces, continually present us with portraits, or rather ghosts of ourselves, which we glance at, and straightway forget them. But we forget them only because they vanish. It is the idea of duration—or earthly immortality—that gives such a mysterious interest to our own portraits (I, 199).

And, indeed, as the painter worked upon their pictures, with a touch applied now to one canvas, now to the other, their features "began to start forth so vividly that it appeared as if his triumphant art would actually disengage them from the canvas. Amid the rich light and deep shade, they beheld their phantom selves" (I, 199). Already the pictures had been given a ghostly life of their own which would vie with that of the living beings from whom the artist had taken the outline and color of his creation. A peculiar circumstance attended the making of the portraits. The artist had originally proposed a single, large painting representing the pair together "in some appropriate action." This idea was necessarily rejected, for the modest home of the couple would not contain sufficient wall space for so large a canvas, and two half-portraits were decided upon instead. Yet the painter had chosen nevertheless to paint the two portraits simultaneously, "assigning as a reason, in the mystical language which he sometimes used, that the faces threw light upon each other" (I, 198).

When the pictures are finally complete, Walter and Elinor detect an unexpected quality in each other's portraits, something added by a last touch between their previous and present visits. The painter's prophetic insight has worked the change; his complete prediction—the act that was to express the change in their personalities—is already depicted in the crayon sketch he shows Elinor. One feels that this sketch has an even more vivid life of its own

than the paintings.[9] It is drawn again by a sensitive viewer
of the portraits—as though the act it represents were a
picture hidden in the painted expressions of Walter and
Elinor, just as their expressions had been hidden in the
appearance they presented to the painter. "Though un-
skilled in the art, he even began a sketch, in which the
action of the two figures was to correspond with their
mutual expression" (I, 204). The final Gothic touch arrives
when Elinor hangs a heavy purple curtain of silk before the
portraits, like the black silk curtain before the mysterious
picture in *The Mysteries of Udolpho.*

Hawthorne is known for his tendency to treat the supernatural with a mocking, only half-serious diffidence, so that
the reader is never quite sure whether symbol or unnatural
fact is being indicated by Donatello's pointed ears or the
fiery "A" glowing in the night sky over Hester's Salem. The
famous question, "Had Goodman Brown fallen asleep in
the forest and only dreamed a wild dream of a witch-meet-
ing?" is never finally answered. So these hints and assertions
about the portraits and their prophetic author seem to suggest that we are dealing with a magician and a magical
work—yet all is within the realm of probability, and an
alternative explanation is available for the objectivist. By
this technique—as in the other instances mentioned—
Hawthorne perhaps accomplishes a particular result. He
gives us the preternatural as a symbol for the unnatural
quality sometimes concealed in the seemingly natural.
This, in the case of the painter of the "prophetic pictures,"
is the hidden perversity of the artist's relationship with the
human subjects of his art.

For the painter has come to identify not the portraits
with their sitters, but the sitters with their portraits. Musing
upon his paintings during his wanderings, he longs to see
the originals again, for, as noted earlier, "So much of himself—of his imagination and all other powers—had been

lavished on the study of Walter and Elinor, that he almost regarded them as creations of his own, like the thousands with which he had peopled the realms of Picture" (I, 206). This is his fatal error and arrogance. After knocking at the door of the doomed pair, he asks involuntarily: "The portraits! Are they within?"—and then corrects himself— "Your master and mistress! Are they at home?" The pictures have indeed absorbed the lives of their subjects like magic Gothic portraits. He comes upon the scene of terror which his prophet's eye had sighted long ago: "In the action, and in the look and attitude of each, the painter beheld the figures of his sketch. The picture, with all its tremendous coloring, was finished" (I, 209).

But Hawthorne sees this appalling consequence not as the result of any unique perversity on the part of the painter, but as the result of the very purity of his aim as an artist. He has come to colonial America for new lessons in the language of art. "America was too poor to afford other temptations," but after studying all that civilized culture had to teach him at home in Europe "till there was nothing more for his powerful mind to learn," he sought a new source of inspiration. "Art could add nothing to its lessons, but Nature might" (I, 194). He was not tempted by wealth or flattered by fame. When some provincial worthy proposed to have his features immortalized by the artist,

He fixed his piercing eyes on the applicant, and seemed to look him through and through. If he beheld only a sleek and comfortable visage, though there were a gold-laced coat to adorn the picture and golden guineas to pay for it, he civilly rejected the task and reward. But if the face were the index of anything uncommon, in thought, sentiment, or experience; or if he met a beggar in the street with a white beard and a furrowed brow; or if sometimes a child happened to look up and smile, he would exhaust all the art on them that he denied to wealth (I, 194-95).

Beholding what he saw with a keenness granted to few men, he possessed the "second sight" of the Romantic artist. He tells Elinor:

> The artist—the true artist—must look beneath the exterior, it is his gift—his proudest, but often melancholy one—to seek the immost soul, and, by a power indefinable even to himself, to make it glow or darken upon the canvas, in glances that express the thought and sentiment of years (I, 202).

Solitary and somber, like one of Byron's heroes, the painter travels into the pathless woodlands of the virgin continent. He sees the "Crystal Hills," the splendor of Lake George and Niagara, the primitive dignity of the Indian and the "old French partisan, bred in courts, but grown gray in shaggy deserts." He feels at last that all of Nature has revealed herself to him, "that the deep wisdom in his art, which he had sought so far, was found" (I, 205). He scorns the meaner minds of ordinary men. Exulting in his art, "with a proud, yet melancholy fervor, did he almost cry aloud, as he passed through the toilsome street, among people that knew not of his reveries, nor could understand nor care for them" (I, 207).

And yet, says Hawthorne,

> It is not good for man to cherish a solitary ambition. Unless there be those around him by whose example he may regulate himself, his thoughts, desires, and hopes will become extravagant, and he the semblance, perhaps the reality, of a madman. Reading other bosoms with an acuteness almost preternatural, the painter failed to see the disorder of his own (I, 207).

So Hawthorne writes the most terrible indictment of the artist's nature that his work contains. The painter of the "prophetic pictures," he tells us, had no kindly feelings; his heart was cold.

Like all other men around whom an engrossing purpose wreathes itself, he was insulated from the mass of human kind. He had no aim—no pleasure—no sympathies—but what were ultimately connected with his art. Though gentle in manner and upright in intent and action, he did not possess kindly feelings; his heart was cold; no living creature could be brought near enough to keep him warm. For these two beings, however, he had felt, in its greatest intensity, the sort of interest which always allied him to the subjects of his pencil. He had pried into their souls with keenest insight, and pictured the result upon their features with his utmost skill, so as barely to fall short of that standard which no genius ever reached, his own severe conception (I, 206).

The Woodcarver Drowne

In "Drowne's Wooden Image," written probably in the same year as "The Artist of the Beautiful,"[10] Hawthorne returned to the colonial scene which had provided background and moral reference for "The Prophetic Pictures." In mood it stands at the opposite end of the scale from the early study of a colonial portrait painter, for its theme is not the alienating effects of art, but the dependence of true genius upon the power of love. In a word, Drowne is not a Faust. He has not exchanged love for art; for him, indeed, art is the result of love, a development of Heart rather than of Head. To Hawthorne's honeymoon in the Old Manse we can attribute, probably, this delicate and tender little piece in which the claims of life and art are not antithetical, but identical. Hardly ever again was Hawthorne's fiction to exhibit this mood, and it is not surprising, as Elizabeth Chandler points out, that there are no Notebook origins for the tale.[11]

The idea of the plot stems, of course, from an older, mellower tradition than Puritan legend. "Who would have looked for a modern Pygmalion in the person of a Yankee mechanic!" (II, 353), exclaims Copley in the story. Hawthorne has taken the classic myth and transmuted it, much as he later did the stories of *A Wonder-Book,* about which he wrote his publisher, James T. Fields: "I shall aim at substituting a tone in some degree Gothic or romantic, or any such tone as may best please myself, instead of the classic coldness, which is as repellent as the touch of marble" (IV, 10). The Gothic aspect of "Drowne's Wooden Image" derives from the motif of the magic art-work discussed above. The painted ship's figurehead that seems to come alive stands in an unhaunted, daylight atmosphere, and is only distantly related to Alfonso's bleeding statue in *The Castle of Otranto.* Yet the Romantic idea that artistic creation is a process mimicking natural creation, and that the work of art has a separate life and power given it by the artist's inspiration, is to some degree involved whenever statues walk or portraits descend from the wall. And Drowne's wooden statue of a beautiful woman is distinctly an art-work animated by the wizard breath of creative ardor.

Playful and dainty as it is, with the seriousness of neither "The Artist of the Beautiful" nor of "The Prophetic Pictures," the story of Drowne the woodcarver is, nevertheless, another analysis of the Romantic theory of art. Briefly, it tells how an adept of the Fancy became a genius of the Imagination. The modest young carver in his Boston workshop is also the prototype of those American sculptors, mentioned previously, who were to occasion so much comment from Hawthorne during his stay in Rome. "He was the first American who is known to have attempted—in a very humble line, it is true—that art in which we can now reckon so many names already distinguished, or rising to distinction" (II, 348). Since boyhood, we are told, he had shown a facility of hand, if not the true quality of inspiration, in fashioning figures of all sorts:

...he had exhibited a knack—for it would be too proud a

word to call it genius—a knack, therefore, for the imitation
of the human figure in whatever material came most readily
to hand. The snows of a New England winter had often supplied him with a species of marble as dazzlingly white, at
least, as the Parian or the Carrara, and if less durable, yet
sufficiently so to correspond with any claims to permanent
existence possessed by the boy's frozen statues. Yet they won
admiration from maturer judges than his school-fellows, and
were indeed remarkably clever, though destitute of the native
warmth that might have made the snow melt beneath his
hand. As he advanced in life, the young man adopted pine
and oak as eligible materials for the display of his skill,
which now began to bring him a return of solid silver as well
as the empty praise that had been an apt reward enough for
his productions of evanescent snow (II, 348-49).

As a manufacturer of ornamental pumpheads, gateposts,
and even staring images for the prows of vessels, Drowne
received deserved applause, though it had to be confessed
that all his figureheads bore a depressing family likeness—
"they all had a kind of wooden aspect which proved an
intimate relationship with the unshaped blocks of timber
in the carver's workshop" (II, 349-50). His works, then,
could be identified as mechanical rather than organic, products of the Fancy instead of the Imagination:

> . . . there was no inconsiderable skill of hand, nor a deficiency
> of any attribute to render them really works of art, except
> that deep quality, be it of soul or intellect, which bestows life
> upon the lifeless and warmth upon the cold, and which, had
> it been present, would have made Drowne's wooden image
> instinct with spirit (II, 350).

The celebrated Copley, stepping into Drowne's shop one
day to admire his countryman's "mechanical and wooden
cleverness," tells him that his images lack "but one touch"
to make them come alive, to turn, as he indicates for an

example, "this figure of General Wolfe . . . into a breathing and intelligent human creature" (II, 352). This theory of the one transforming touch is a recognizable and highly significant Romanticism. Not the cumulative results of craft, but a single alteration prompted by forces inaccessible to ordinary calculation, will turn the inanimate into the animate. Drowne admits that "the one touch which you speak of as deficient is the only one that would be truly valuable, and without it these works of mine are no better than worthless abortions" (II, 352). The touch they refer to is, of course, the stroke of the magician's wand—in other words, a piece of occultism—and so it is not surprising that the metaphor of its effects is that of a carven image starting to life. Drowne's ordinary work looked as though the living subject had been reduced to inanimate substance rather than as though the inert wood had seized the life of the breathing model,

> as if a living man had here been changed to wood, and that not only the physical, but the intellectual and spiritual part, partook of the stolid transformation. But in not a single instance did it seem as if the wood were imbibing the ethereal essence of humanity. What a wide distinction is here! and how far would the slightest portion of the latter merit have outvalued the utmost degree of the former! (II, 351)

But Copley turns suddenly to a half-finished piece of work standing in a corner of Drowne's shop—the female figurehead which the carver has been shaping for the brig *Cynosure* under commission from her owner and commander, Captain Hunnewell. "What is here? Who has done this?" he cries. "Here is the divine, the life-giving touch. What inspired hand is beckoning this wood to arise and live?" (II, 353)

That Drowne is now involved in the ancient and mysterious act of creating a "living" work of art, is obscurely recognized by observers. As the chips scatter about the emerging form, "it seemed as if the hamadryad of the oak had sheltered herself from the unimaginative world within the heart of her native tree, and that it was only necessary to remove the strange shapelessness that had incrusted her to reveal the grace and loveliness of a divinity" (II, 351). "Gradually, by a magic touch, intelligence and sensibility brightened through the features, with all the effect of light gleaming forth from within the solid oak. The face became alive" (II, 354). Soon she was complete—colored in the hues of nature, a "richly-dressed and beautiful young lady who seemed to stand in a corner of the room, with oaken chips and shavings scattered at her feet" (II, 356).

As a miracle or a work of magic should, the phenomenon of such art arouses tumultuous feelings. "Then came a sensation of fear; as if, not being actually human, yet so like humanity, she must therefore be something supernatural" (II, 356). The more bigoted of Drowne's neighbors hint that an evil spirit is likely enough the inhabitant of this beautiful form. And then one day the magic transformation of wood to flesh actually takes place—or seems to. "Drowne's wooden image has come to life!" cry the passers-by as she steps along the street. They do not know "whether to suppose the magic wood etherealized into a spirit or warmed and softened into an actual woman," but "one thing is certain," mutters a Puritan of the old stamp, "Drowne has sold himself to the devil . . ." (II, 359). Here is just the slightest, lightest hint of the Faust compact as a symbol for the occult nature of the artist's inspiration, but Drowne, unlike the painter of the "prophetic pictures," is only temporarily and accidentally in contact with the supernatural powers that seem so diabolic in the painter's case. And, unlike Owen, Drowne pays no penalty for his involvement with the nonhuman spirit world, which he has achieved, for a wonderful, single moment, not by renouncing love but by succumbing to it.[12]

As usual, Hawthorne has at hand a rational explanation —for those who feel the need of one. The living young lady who had posed for Drowne was a young Portuguese beauty under Captain Hunnewell's protection—and so on. But the effect of the Pygmalion motif—the Gothic statue come alive —still remains. For *art,* as the story romantically defines it, *is* a miracle. "Whose work is this?" asks Copley, "No man's work," replies Drowne. "The figure lies within that block of oak, and it is my business to find it" (II, 353). Platonically he must find the pure form of beauty inherent in nature. Not his own effort, but some sweeping power greater than himself, like the demon of inspiration that the Greeks spoke of, takes possession of the artist's soul. Thus, like Ion the rhapsode, or a spiritualist medium, Drowne describes his experience: "A well-spring of inward wisdom gushed within me as I wrought upon the oak with my whole strength, and soul and faith" (II, 355). When the seizure is over the possessed one cannot explain his performance.

> Drowne looked at him with a visage that bore the traces of tears, but from which the light of imagination and sensibility, so recently illuminating it, had departed. He was again the mechanical carver that he had been known to be all his lifetime.
>
> "I hardly understand what you mean, Mr. Copley," said he, putting his hand to his brow. "This image! Can it have been my work? Well, I have wrought it in a kind of dream; and now that I am broad awake I must set about finishing yonder figure of Admiral Vernon" (II, 361).

As Hawthorne explains it, the miracle has been wrought by love. Copley observes the carver stretching his arms toward the image in a gesture of embrace, his countenance expressing more than aesthetic passion, and others must have seen the same, for some gossiping Bostonians report that Drowne is wont to gaze "with a lover's passionate ardor into the face his own hands had created" (II, 357); and Drowne calls her "this creature of my heart" (II, 355). But it is love for a living woman, for the model, not the statue, which has put into Drowne's face that "expression of human love which in a spiritual sense, as the artist could not help imagining, was the secret of the life that has been breathed into this block of wood" (II, 355). Simple Drowne has been kindled by love of the mysterious visitor from Fayal who is to sail away again in the ship for whose figurehead she had posed in his little shop.

Hawthorne, describing now the statue and now the lady, paints an unforgettable picture of this creature. She is a true sister of Zenobia, even to the "rich, strange flowers of Eden on her head; her complexion, so much deeper and more brilliant than those of our native beauties," the dark eyes and voluptuous mouth, the sumptuous and slightly fantastic clothing—an image of feminine allure that held Hawthorne first and last and created his most memorable female characters—Beatrice Rappaccini, Hester, Zenobia, and Miriam. And being like them, she suggests experience, that night journey which the man who would be an artist must take. She suggests knowledge, the ambiguous fruit gained only through experience, which is the creative intellect's desire. And she suggests, too, sin, the moral cost of experience and knowledge, which is the artist's peril. But these suggestions, which are so strong in Hawthorne's other studies of her, hardly make themselves felt in this most fleeting appearance of his "dark lady." Drowne's idealized love has created for him no permanent implication in the powers and penalties she represents. And so, unlike Owen Warland or the painter of the "prophetic pictures," he is only once an artist.

We have seen elsewhere Hawthorne's somber reflections concerning the effect of art upon the emotions, but in this story he asserted his belief that the greatest art is the product of love—not for a cold ideal, but for a human reality. By means of love's magic all may rise to the height of art.

> In every human spirit there is imagination, sensibility, creative genius, which, according to circumstances, may either be developed in this world, or shrouded in a mask of dullness until another state of being. . . . To our friend Drowne there came a brief season of excitement, kindled by love. It rendered him a genius for one occasion, but, quenched in disappointment, left him again the mechanical carver in wood, without the power even of appreciating the work that his own hands had wrought (II, 362).

And yet, he did not dare give Drowne a further experience of artistic achievement, it almost seems. He did not dare test the union of love and art by longer trial. Surely it is significant that while "Drowne's Wooden Image" relates a remarkable episode in an ordinary life, "The Prophetic Pictures" and "The Artist of the Beautiful" allegorize the effects of the artist's lifetime compact.

NOTES TO CHAPTER V

[1] "The Prophetic Pictures" was published in 1837 in the *Token*, a Boston annual.

[2] *A History of the Rise and Development of the Arts of Design in the United States* (New York: G. P. Scott & Co., 1834), I, 187.

[3] *Selected Short Stories* (New York: Alfred A. Knopf, 1946), pp. xi-xii.

[4] Warren has suggested that the colonial painter John Smibert was the prototype of Hawthorne's character (cf. *Nathaniel Hawthorne*, p. 366), but I think any such resemblance must be accidental, for if the

painter of the prophetic portraits had any prototype at all, it was one hidden in the recesses of the author's own soul.

5 *Biographia Literaria,* ed. John Shawcross (Oxford: The Clarendon Press, 1907), I, 202.

6 "The sign and credentials of the poet are that he announces that which no man foretold. He is the true and only doctor; he knows and tells; he is the only one teller of news, for he was present and privy to the appearance which he describes" ("The Poet," *Works,* VIII). Cf. Carlyle: "Prophet and Poet . . . have much kindred of meaning. Fundamentally indeed they are still the same; in . . . that they have penetrated both of them into the sacred mystery of the Universe; what Goethe calls 'the open secret' . . . that divine mystery which lies everywhere in all beings" ("Heroes and Hero-Worship," *Works,* V, 80); and "The true Poet is ever, as of old, the Seer; whose eye has been gifted to discern the godlike Mystery of God's Universe; and decipher some new lines of its celestial writing; we can still call him *Vates* and Seer; for he *sees* into this greatest of secrets, 'the open secret'; hidden things become clear; how the Future (both resting on Eternity) is but another phase of the present; thereby are his words in very truth prophetic; what he has spoken shall be done" ("Death of Goethe," *ibid.,* XXVII, 377).

7 "Romanticism: A Symposium," *PMLA,* LV (1940), 26.

8 Cf. Friedrich von Schlegel: "We must be able to rise above our own love; in our thoughts we must be able to destroy what we worship; otherwise no matter what other capacities we have, we lack a sense of the infinite and of the world." Quoted by J. C. Blankenagel in *ibid.,* p. 7.

9 See above, Chapter II.

10 "Drowne's Wooden Image" appeared in *Godey's Magazine,* July, 1844.

11 "Tales and Romances by Nathaniel Hawthorne," *Smith College Studies in Modern Languages,* VII, No. 4 (July, 1926), 35.

12 So one cannot really regard Drowne as one of Hawthorne's Fausts. One certainly cannot do so by reversing the traditional sense of the Faust compact—a bargain for occult powers—as does Stein, who suggests that in invoking the image of the devil, Hawthorne's purpose is "to symbolize the disparaging demon of modern life that holds inspiration to be a thing of suspicion," and that when Drowne attains his single inspiration he does so by repelling the influence of the demon (*Hawthorne's Faust,* pp. 96-97). It is for no average happiness, modest and unambitious, that a Faust bargains, but for the opportunity to exceed other men, even at the price of what they call happiness.

Chapter VI

Oberon: *the Mask of*
Nathaniel Hawthorne

~~~~~~

During the thirties, Hawthorne published a group of sketches—chiefly in the *Token* and the *New England Magazine*—which featured a peculiarly personal type of author-character. Sometimes he is an obvious surrogate for Hawthorne, the essayist's scarcely obtrusive "I," as in the travel descriptions based on walking jaunts through rural New England. Occasionally he is a distinctly modeled personality, like the Oberon of "The Devil in Manuscript" and the "Fragments from the Journal of a Solitary Man." In almost all of the score of sketches to be discussed now, however, touches accumulate toward a definite portrait. Its subject is a solitary, introspective writer who observes the procession of the active world from some hidden coign of vantage, peopling his loneliness with imaginary fancies, and seeking Fame as a bride. Yet his way of life fills him with a sense of guilt. He longs wistfully for the warmth of common affections and the love of a simple heart. As to Faust in the old chapbook stories, these are denied him by the terms of his bond. To win them he must surrender his art.

The pieces in this group are probably the most autobiographic of all Hawthorne's imaginative works, and have been widely used by his biographers to give account of the writer's feelings during the so-called "lonely chamber" period—that stretch (1825-37) which lies between his graduation from college and the publication of *Twice-Told Tales*. Now, of course, all Hawthorne's artist-portraits have a more direct biographical bearing, it may be assumed, than his portraits of other characters. But having said this much, we should probably stop right here, acknowledging our inability to determine how much or how little of his creator's nature is embodied in any one of these figures. Oberon, the artist-figure of Hawthorne's early sketches, does bear the name Hawthorne used in college in signing letters to Horatio Bridge, his closest friend. But he is probably no more certainly autobiographic in essential characteristics than those opposites, Owen Warland and the artist of the "prophetic pictures," who by their very difference remind us of the impossibility of discovering direct self-portraiture in either.

So, despite a number of autobiographical suggestions, often noted—for example, that Oberon, like his creator, threw into his fire a mass of unpublished manuscripts on which he had spent long hours of lonely toil—we must, I think, resist the impulse to regard him as a portrait of the young artist Hawthorne. Oberon is merely the first of Hawthorne's significant masks, the "I"-character who is only another of the writer's creations. Even the narrating "I" of the early tales or sketches is identified with Hawthorne at our peril. If he is psychologically true to Hawthorne at all, he is true in the sense of being a self he proposed to himself, a self he tested and considered as a possibility of himself, even a self he sentimentally liked to pretend that he was when depicting himself to others. He does resemble, somewhat, the rather languishing image that Hawthorne offered up to Sophia in his famous letters of courtship. But this image too has often been challenged as only a partial truth—a literary creation in itself, motivated, no doubt, by the lover's anxiety to testify to the transforming effect of the love his sweetheart had aroused in him.

What the real Hawthorne was like modern biography has not always found it easy to say, though some more conclusive picture may be drawn from all his writings, literary and nonliterary, notebooks and fiction taken together, than from any single biographic-seeming figure in his stories. I shall suggest, in a final chapter, my own view of that last, ungraspable image, that of the vanished man himself, the man who created all his legends of art and artists, and stood apart from them, too. What is more valuable and interesting for us to view here, however, is the symbolic function of this early artist-personality who appears in his writing. He may partly be the product of Hawthorne's own career, which through a dozen years had still yielded no public recognition and little monetary reward. He is, also, already the result of a complicated cultural history by which the idealist renunciation of the materialist world had begun to seem to critics like Hawthorne either an involuntary exile or a perverse withdrawal from normal human bonds. Hawthorne's first published work, the novel *Fanshawe,* is a Romantic depiction of the fate of the Romantic poet. In these sketches, which with the early stories form our next evidence of Hawthorne's mental growth, the artist-figure is reviewed again and again in terms of Fanshawe's alternatives—the world and the ideal. But the artist of the sketches is already a figure tinged with associations of moral disease, unlike the pure-minded Fanshawe. He is the lineal forebear of the artist of "The Prophetic Pictures."

The most fully developed of these portraits is the writer Oberon, who appears in two pieces, "The Devil in Manuscript" and the "Fragments from the Journal of a Solitary Man." The first of these, published in the *New England Magazine* in November, 1835, sketches the character of

Oberon, the young story writer, "one of those gifted youths who cultivate poetry and the *belles lettres,* and call themselves students at law" (III, 574). He reminds us not so much of Hawthorne himself as of the whole generation of young intellectuals who were sent into business or the law although their talents disposed them to the arts.[1] Oberon is discovered in the act of burning his manuscripts, in which, as he says, a devil is concealed. He explains that he means "that conception in which I endeavored to embody the character of a fiend, as represented in our traditions and the written records of witchcraft" (III, 575). But the whimsy of a "conception" half conceals Hawthorne's suggestion that Oberon is ridden by a literal fiend, whom only fire can exorcise. For in a moment the fictional demon becomes identified with the writer's "possession" by his art, with the tales themselves, which he must commit to the flames:

> You remember . . . how the hellish thing used to suck away the happiness of those who, by a simple concession that seemed almost innocent, subjected themselves to his power. Just so my peace is gone, and all by these accursed manuscripts. . . . You cannot conceive what an effect the composition of these tales has had on me. I have become ambitious of a bubble, and careless of solid reputation. I am surrounding myself with shadows, which bewilder me by aping the realities of life. They have drawn me aside from the beaten path of the world, and led me into a strange sort of solitude, —a solitude in the midst of men,—where nobody wishes for what I do, nor thinks nor feels as I do. The tales have done all this. When they are ashes, perhaps I shall be as I was before they had existence (III, 575-76).

Oberon assures his friend that this exorcism by fire will hardly be a sacrifice, since nobody has consented to publish his productions:

They have been offered, by letter ... to some seventeen book-sellers. It would make you stare to read their answers: and read them you should, only that I burnt them as fast as they arrived. One man publishes nothing but school-books; another has five novels already under examination ... another gentleman is just giving up business, on purpose, I verily believe, to escape publishing my book. Several, however, would not absolutely decline the agency, on my advancing half the cost of an edition, and giving bonds for the remainder, besides a high percentage to themselves, whether the book sells or not. Another advises a subscription. ... In short, of all the seventeen booksellers, only one has vouchsafed even to read my tales; and he—a literary dabbler himself, I should judge —has the impertinence to criticize them, proposing what he calls vast improvements, and concluding, after a general sentence of condemnation, with the definitive assurance that he will not be concerned on any terms. ... If the whole 'trade' had one common nose, there would be some satisfaction in pulling it. ... But there does seem to be one honest man among these seventeen unrighteous ones; and he tells me fairly, that no American publisher will meddle with an American work; seldom if by a known writer, and never if by a new one,—unless at the writer's risk (III, 576-77).

The two passages above represent two important aspects of Hawthorne's speculation. The second gives us a scathing circumstantial picture of the condition of publishing in America in his time. The first, however, is more important, for it displays Hawthorne's fears that the practice of art itself may be pernicious because it makes the artist careless of the solid realities of life and draws him away from the beaten path of the world. His Oberon declares that art makes outlaws of its votaries:

I will burn them! Not a scorched syllable shall escape. Would you have me a damned author?—to undergo sneers, taunts, abuse, and cold neglect, and faint praise, bestowed, for pity's sake, and against the giver's conscience! A hissing and a laughing stock to my own traitorous thoughts! An outlaw from the protection of the grave,—one whose ashes every careless foot might spurn, unhonored in life, and remembered scornfully in death! (III, 580)

But what remains to Oberon, now that he has destroyed the creation of long nights and days? "A weary aimless life, —a long repentance of this hour, and at last an obscure grave, where they will bury and forget me" (II, 582).

Hawthorne concludes the sketch with humorous exuberance: the fire his hero's manuscripts lit in the chimney has leapt out upon the neighboring houses; the alarm cry of "Fire!" rings through the town. Oberon hears the bells of the engines. "And that other sound, too—deep and awful as a mighty organ,—the roar and thunder of the multitude on the pavement below! Come! We are losing time. I will cry out in the loudest of the uproar, and mingle my spirit with the wildest of the confusion and be a bubble on the top of the ferment!" (II, 583). And so in his immolation he attains that union with a multitude for which he longs.

Oberon appeared again in the "Fragments from the Journal of a Solitary Man," which was published in the *American Monthly Magazine* in July, 1837. Here the allegory of the artist's life is more completely represented. The dying Oberon regrets the life which has severed him from earthly pains and satisfaction—the artist's detachment which forbids him either to suffer or rejoice with other men:

It is hard to die without one's happiness; to none more so than myself, whose early resolution it had been to partake largely of the joys of life, but never to be burdened with its cares. Vain philosophy! The very hardship of the poorest laborer, whose whole existence seems one long toil, has something preferable to my best pleasures.

Merely skimming the surface of life, I know nothing, by

my own experience, of its deep and warm realities. I have achieved none of these objects which the instinct of mankind especially prompts them to pursue, and the accomplishment of which must therefore beget a native satisfaction. The truly wise, after all their speculations, will be led into the common path, and, in homage to the human nature that pervades them, will gather gold, and till the earth, and set out trees, and build a house. But I have scorned such wisdom. I have rejected, also, the settled, sober, careful gladness of a man by his own fireside, with those around him whose welfare is committed to his trust, and all their guidance to his fond authority. Without influence among serious affairs, my footsteps were not imprinted on the earth, but lost in air; and I shall leave no son to inherit my share in life, with a better sense of its privileges and duties, when his father should vanish like a bubble; so that few mortals, even the humblest and the weakest, have been such ineffectual shadows in the world, or die so utterly as I must. Even a young man's bliss has not been mine. With a thousand vagrant fantasies, I have never truly loved, and perhaps shall be doomed to loneliness throughout the eternal future, because, here on earth, my soul has never married itself to the soul of woman.

Such are the repinings of one who feels, too late, that the sympathies of his nature have avenged themselves upon him. They have prostrated, with a joyless life and the prospect of a reluctant death, my selfish purpose to keep aloof from mortal disquietudes, and be a pleasant idler among care-stricken and laborious men (XII, 25-26).

In this passage Oberon does more than repine over the conventional melancholy lot of the Romantic artist. His censure springs from Hawthorne's deep humanist sense of the values of sociality. The "deep and warm realities," the "common path," the "gladness of a man by his own fireside," and, finally, the love of woman—these are the life-values which Hawthorne poses against the spiritual exaltation of the lonely seeker. It is the fundamental antithesis of Hawthorne's thinking about the artist. We have seen that the division it represents renders the heart of the painter of the "prophetic pictures" cold and self-absorbed; Owen Warland found it impossible both to attain his vision of the Beautiful and to keep a place for himself at the warm hearth of human affections. Such, exactly, is the problem set before the three artist-heroes of the novels—Coverdale, Holgrave, and Kenyon—as we shall see in the next chapter.

Oberon's musing in the "Journal of a Solitary Man" introduces two of Hawthorne's persistent themes: a longing for "our old home" and a desire for perpetual life. He remarks that he had long hoped to "return, as it were, to my home of past ages, and see the very cities, and castles, and battle-fields of history, and stand within the holy gloom of its cathedrals, and kneel at the shrines of its immortal poets, there asserting myself their hereditary countryman" (XII, 26). Another obsession had been his fear of old age—"the terrible necessity imposed on mortals to grow old, or die" (XII, 27). These twin themes are the preoccupation of the unfinished romances that Hawthorne struggled with at the end of his life. It is interesting to see how, even at this early point, they are connected with his speculations concerning the artist's character and fate. Nostalgia for the European homeland is an impulse that anticipates the experience of Henry James, Henry Adams, and T. S. Eliot. It is, indeed, representative of the American artist's persistent suspicion that the cultural continuity of which he wishes to be a part is only to be found in the intellectual capitals of the world —Paris, London, Rome—away from the unordered American scene. The desire for an extension of youth also stems from a sense of lifelong artistic frustration—"I am possessed, also, with the thought that I have never yet discovered the real secret of my powers," declares Oberon (XII, 27). We have seen how Owen Warland longed for such a further grant of time in his endeavors to achieve the

Beautiful. Septimius Felton also has an ideal aim which causes him to desire the elixir of perpetual life. In addition, Hawthorne gives another reason: the life of the artist is unsuited to age. "In his old age the sweet lyrics of Anacreon made the girls laugh at his white hairs the more." On the other hand: "He who has a part in the serious business of life, though it be only as a shoemaker, feels himself equally respectable in youth and age, and therefore is content to live and look forward to wrinkles and decrepitude in their due season" (XII, 28).

"My Home Return," an excerpt from Oberon's "journal," is the touching account of the prodigal's return to his native village. "Why have I never loved my home before?" he asks, as he views the simple mirth of the villagers. He looks among them for a youth, minded, as he was once, to set off from such a scene in pursuit of the snow-capped ridges of art.

> He shall be taught . . . by my life and by my death, that the world is a sad one for him who shrinks from its sober duties. My experience shall warn him to adopt some great and serious aim such as manhood will cling to, that he may not feel himself, too late, a cumberer of the overladen earth, but a man among men. I will beseech him not to follow an eccentric path, nor, by stepping aside from the highway of human affairs, to relinquish his claim upon human sympathy. And often, as a text of deep and varied meaning, I will remind him that he is an American (XII, 40).

At one time, Hawthorne planned a collection of pieces to be called *The Story Teller,* which would connect some of the stories he had written by a narrative frame—an account of the wanderings of a young raconteur who recites his yarns to New England village audiences. The storyteller was to be another version of Oberon, an artist who discovers that the ordinary round of life holds no attraction for him, and that the pursuits that do appeal to him are censured by his world. He wanders far from his native New England village, following the dictates of his own whim and rejecting the sober path of modest content. His self-description in "Passages from a Relinquished Work," which appeared in the *New England Magazine* in November and December, 1834, is of great significance:

> I, being heir to a moderate competence, had avowed my purpose of keeping aloof from the regular business of life. This would have been a dangerous resolution anywhere in the world; it was fatal in New England. There is a grossness in the conceptions of my countrymen; they will not be convinced that any good thing may consist in what they call idleness; they can anticipate nothing but evil of a young man who neither studies physic, law, nor gospel, nor opens a store, nor takes to farming but manifests an incomprehensible disposition to be satisfied with what his father left him. I had a quick sensitiveness to public opinion, and felt as if it ranked me with the tavern haunters and town paupers,—with the drunken poet who hawked his own Fourth of July odes, and the broken soldier who had been good for nothing since last war (II, 459).

So, like Oberon, he leaves his familiar natal village behind, and sets forth upon his rambles. His mood is cheerful; never, he declares, "was Childe Harold's sentiment adopted in a spirit more unlike his own" (II, 463). And yet the note of guilt and exile is not long in arriving. A letter follows him, written by the stern guardian who had nurtured him, but the young man burns it unread.

> It is fixed in my mind, and was so at the time, that he had addressed me in a style of paternal wisdom, and love, and reconciliation, which I could not have resisted had I but risked the trial. The thought still haunts me that then I made my irrevocable choice between good and evil fate (II, 475).

In the *Token,* the year before, Hawthorne introduced this wandering storyteller in the company of a group of itinerant entertainers on their way to the camp meeting at Stamford. He proposes to go along with them and try his art. But suddenly he asks himself:

> How come I among these wanderers? The free mind that preferred its own folly to another's wisdom; the open spirit, that found companions everywhere; above all, the restless impulse, that had so often made me wretched in the midst of enjoyments; these were my claims to be of their society (I, 409).

The artist is one who chooses an "evil fate"; he is a vagabond who belongs among the wanderers of the earth.

"The Village Uncle," which was included in the *Token* in 1835, is another full-length, first-person story of the Oberon-storyteller character, but here Hawthorne has exhibited the alternative retrospect of an artist who has chosen to give up his isolating role in exchange for the happiness of the average man. The Village Uncle, seated at his bright hearth with his wife Susan and his children, glimpses back fifty years to discover his pale, younger self at his writing desk, and declares:

> I should be loath to lose my treasure of past happiness, and become once more what I was then; a hermit in the depths of my own mind; sometimes yawning over drowsy volumes, and anon a scribbler of wearier trash than what I read; a man who had wandered out of the real world and got into its shadow, where his troubles, joys and vicissitudes were of such slight stuff that he hardly knew whether he lived, or only dreamed of living (I, 350).

But now he lives with his Susan in the seaside village (which is probably Swampscott, where Hawthorne did once pass-

ingly fall in love with just such a village maid). He has
lived as a fisherman, drawn red rock cod, long-bearded hake,
and haddock, bearing the mark of St. Peter's fingers near
the gills, into his skiff. Winning Susan, he has built a cot-
tage, bought a heifer, and ornamented their parlor with
shells from the beach. Except for the Bible, Susan's singing
book, and the almanac, they have no literature.

> All that I heard of books was when an Indian history, or tale
> of shipwreck, was sold by a pedlar or wandering subscription
> man, to someone in the village, and read through its owner's
> nose to a slumberous auditory. Like my brother fishermen,
> I grew into the belief that all human erudition was collected
> in our pedagogue, whose green spectacles and solemn phiz, as
> he passed to his little school-house amid a waste of sand,
> might have gained him diploma from any college in New
> England. In truth I dreaded him. When our children were
> old enough to claim his care, you remember, Susan, how I
> frowned, though you were pleased, at this learned man's en-
> comiums on their proficiency. I feared to trust them even
> with the alphabet; it was the key to a fatal treasure (I, 357).

So now, venerable, a spinner of yarns and a cherisher of
local traditions, he sits among his descendants, while
memory causes the firelight to glimmer on the walls of the
vanished room "and show the book that I flung down and
the sheet that I left half-written, some fifty years ago." The
moral: "In chaste and warm affections, humble wishes, and
honest toil for some useful end there is health for the mind
and quiet for the heart, the prospect of a happy life, and the
fairest hope of heaven" (I, 363).

This is the pastoral alternative that represents the artist's
salvation—more often rejected—in Hawthorne's fiction.
It is the ironic opportunity of the young idealist of "The
Threefold Destiny," who finds the great promise of
treasure, public office, and high love realized only in the

humble village from which he had started on his quest. It is the same ideal of humble truth that discovers in Ernest, the boy of humble birth and little education, a truer image of the Great Stone Face than in miser, soldier, politician— and poet. The poet himself recognizes that in Ernest's crude eloquence there is "a nobler strain of poetry than any he had ever written." It is this alternative, as we shall see, that, in the lives of Kenyon and Holgrave, finally replaces the ideal of art.

Hawthorne's sketches reveal some of the traits that he identified with the artist-character, particularly the habit of observation, which, as we know he once remarked, has a tendency to "put ice in the blood." In a number of the sketches we encounter an artist-voyeur who observes life from a steeple, or from behind a window curtain. The narrator of "Sights from a Steeple," which the *Token* carried in 1831, declares, as he surveys the roofs of the town from his eminence:

> Oh that the Limping Devil of Le Sage would perch beside me here, extend his wand over this contiguity of roofs, uncover every chamber, and make me familiar with their inhabitants! The most desirable mode of existence might be that of a spiritualized Paul Pry, hovering invisible round man and woman, witnessing their deeds, seaching into their hearts, borrowing brightness from their felicity and shade from their sorrow, and retaining no emotion peculiar to himself (I, 220).

An ideal station of vantage might be that of the toll-gatherer whose day Hawthorne describes in "The Toll-Gatherer's Day":

> Methinks, for a person whose instinct bids him rather to pore over the current of life than to plunge into its tumultuous waves, no undesirable retreat were a toll-house beside some

thronged thoroughfare of the land ... there are natures too indolent, or too sensitive, to endure the dust, the sunshine, or the rain, the turmoil of moral and physical elements, to which all the wayfarers of the world expose themselves. For such a man, how pleasant a miracle, could life be made to roll its variegated length by the threshold of his own hermitage, and the great globe, as it were, perform its revolutions and shift its thousand scenes before his eyes without whirling him onward in its course (I, 234).

Such is the practice of the watcher in "Sunday at Home," who states, "I love to spend such pleasant Sabbaths, from morning till night, behind the curtain of my open window" (I, 34) .

The subject of the artist's dilemma lies obscurely behind most of the sketches of this period, in which Hawthorne seems to speak in his own voice, that of a solitary young writer who faces a choice between the fates of Oberon and the Village Uncle. As he returns from his stroll with little Annie, in "Little Annie's Ramble," he remarks, "I have gone too far astray for the town crier to call me back" (I, 152). In such a purely descriptive piece as "Rochester" among the "Sketches from Memory," he comments upon the daring—and fatal—leap of Sam Patch into the Niagara cataract, and adds:

Was the leaper of the cataract more mad or foolish than other men who throw away life, or misspend it in pursuit of empty fame, and seldom so triumphantly as he? That which he won is as invaluable as any except the unsought glory, spreading like the rich perfume of richer fruit from various and useful deeds. . . .

Thus musing, wise in theory, but practically as great a fool as Sam, I lifted my eyes and beheld the spires, warehouses, and dwellings of Rochester ... (XII, 18).

Regarding the appearance of Monsieur du Miroir in the

mirror, the speaker says, "I involuntarily pursue him as a record of my heavy youth, which has been wasted in sluggishness for lack of hope or impulse, or equally thrown away in toil that had no wise motive and accomplished no good end" (II, 182). And the narrator of "Night Sketches: Beneath an Umbrella" observes that he has been impelled upon this nocturnal stroll "to satisfy myself that the world is not entirely made up of such shadowy materials as have busied me throughout the day. A dreamer may dwell so long among fantasies, that the things without him will seem as unreal as those within" (I, 478).

In "Footprints on the Sea-Shore," this same individual wanders out along the shore for a daytime stroll to enjoy the solitude of the beach, but when a party frying fish upon the shingle hails him with jolly shouts of "Haloo, Sir Solitary, come down and sup with us!" he admits that "after all my solitary joys . . . this is the sweetest moment of a day by the Sea-Shore" (I, 516). He might, after all, like the Village Uncle, meet the Susan who would lead his footsteps into the path of common joy.

NOTE TO CHAPTER VI

[1] Hawthorne's fellow townsman, William Wetmore Story, was to practice law for six years and publish a two-volume treatise on the law of contracts and other legal works before he exchanged Salem for Italy and the arts.

Chapter VII

The Artists of the Novels:

Coverdale, Holgrave, Kenyon

~~~~~~

The artist-hero appears in three of Hawthorne's four novels. Coverdale the poet, Holgrave the story writer and photographer, and Kenyon the sculptor represent Hawthorne's most mature formulations of the artistic character. It will be seen that these three artists are direct developments of the narrator-artist Oberon, of the sketches, and still act as authorial witnesses. This is most clearly true of Miles Coverdale in *The Blithedale Romance,* which alone among Hawthorne's longer fictional works is written in the first person. Both Holgrave and Kenyon, however, retain some of the narrator's function in their respective novels, and we observe the action and the other characters from viewpoints fairly close to theirs. As a result, we get more intense inner pictures of these artist-personalities than we do of the surrounding personages; they are Hawthorne's most "psychological" characters.

Miles Coverdale is the most fully explored character in *The Blithedale Romance,* though he takes no real part in the growth of the action. He is not merely the narrator of the story, for it sometimes seems that the story itself exists as much to show us the nature of the storyteller as for its own sake. It is against the action that we judge Coverdale, measuring him in turn by Hollingsworth's idealism, Zenobia's intensity, and Priscilla's innocence.

In *The Blithedale Romance* the artist is viewed in terms of progressive self-disclosure. Coverdale comes to Blithedale with the finest of romantic notions about his worth as a poet. On his first evening at Blithedale he declares:

> I . . . hope now to produce something that shall really deserve to be called poetry,—true, strong, natural, and sweet, as is the life which we are going to lead, something that shall have the notes of birds twittering through it, or a strain like the wind-anthems in the woods, as the case may be (V, 336).

But when the story he relates is at an end, Coverdale admits himself to be a failure both in life and art. He has lost a sense of purpose.

> As for poetry, I have given it up, notwithstanding that Dr. Griswold—as the reader, of course, knows—has placed me at a fair elevation among our minor minstrelsy, on the strength of my pretty little volume, published ten years ago. . . . I lack a purpose. . . . I by no means wish to die. Yet were there any cause, in this whole chaos of human struggle worth a sane man's dying for, and which my death would benefit, then—provided, however, the effort did not involve an unreasonable amount of trouble—methinks I might be bold to offer up my life. If Kossuth, for example, would pitch the battlefield of Hungarian rights within an easy ride of my abode, and choose a mild, sunny morning, after breakfast, for the conflict, Miles Coverdale would gladly be his man, for one brave rush upon the levelled bayonets. Further than that, I should be loath to pledge myself (V, 599).

Coverdale traverses the course from illusion to cynicism as the drama of his Blithedale companions reveals his own ineffectual role in life. More and more he finds himself involved in the part of a voyeur; like the narrator of "Sights from a Steeple," he observes his fellow Blithedalers from a sort of crow's-nest elevated above the pains and ardors of normal men and women. Indeed, it does not take him long to find a literal eyrie to symbolize his detached interest in his neighbors. In the wood adjacent to Blithedale he discovers "a kind of leafy cave, high upward into the air, among the midmost branches of a white-pine tree . . . a perfect nest for Robinson Crusoe or King Charles!" (V, 431). And from this natural turret he is wont to peep upon the oblivious companions of his Blithedale adventure.

> . . . my position was lofty enough to serve as an observatory, not for starry investigations, but for those sublunary matters in which lay a lore as infinite as that of the planets. Through one loophole I saw the river lapsing calmly onward, while in the meadow, near its brink, a few of the brethren were digging peat for our winter's fuel. On the interior cart-road of our farm, I discerned Hollingsworth, with a yoke of oxen hitched to a drag of stones. . . . The harsh tones of his voice, shouting to the sluggish steers, made me sensible, even at such a distance, that he was ill at ease. . . . "Mankind, in Hollingsworth's opinion," thought I, "is but another yoke of oxen, as stubborn, stupid, and sluggish as our old Brown and Bright. He vituperates us aloud, and curses us in his heart, and will begin to prick us with the goad stick by and by. . . . At my height above the earth the whole matter looks ridiculous!" (V, 432-33)

Seeing his friend Hollingsworth from this height, he is unmoved by his philanthropic schemes—and that is well enough. But his hidden vantage point gives him also a detached perspective of Priscilla, whom he spots at a window in the farmhouse. To a passing bird he sends an imaginary message:

> "Tell her . . . that her fragile thread of life has inextricably knotted itself with other and tougher threads, and most likely

it will be broken. Tell her that Zenobia will not be long her friend. Say that Hollingsworth's heart is on fire with his own purpose, but icy for all human affection; and that, if she has given him her love, it is like casting a flower into a sepulchre. And say that if any mortal really cares for her, it is myself; and not even I, for her realities,—poor little seamstress, as Zenobia rightly called her!—but for the fancy-work with which I have idly decked her out!" (V, 433-34)

It is the fiery Zenobia who first becomes aware of the peculiar nature of Coverdale's observation. One day, as she feels his speculative glance, she declares:

"Mr. Coverdale . . . I have been exposed to a great deal of eye-shot in the few years of my mixing in the world, but never, I think, to precisely such glances as you are in the habit of favoring me with. I seem to interest you very much; and yet—or else a woman's instinct is for once deceived—I cannot reckon you as an admirer. What are you seeking to discover in me?" (V, 373-74)

He is always fingering and teasing the sensibilities of his friends—trying to make them give up their secrets. As he slyly questions Priscilla, for example, he reflects, "No doubt it was a kind of sacrilege in me to attempt to come within her maidenly mystery; but, as she appeared to be tossed aside by her other friends, or carelessly let fall, like a flower which they had done with, I could not resist the impulse to take just one peep beneath her folded petals" (V, 463). He feels the prompting of curiosity before all other emotions. After terminating his interview in the woods with the detestable Westervelt, he reminds himself that he might have learned something from this diabolic personage: "I could not help regretting that I had so preëmptorily broken off the interview, while the stranger seemed inclined to continue it. His evident knowledge of matters affecting my three friends might have led to disclosures or inferences that would perhaps have been serviceable" (V, 429). Later, in his attempt to discover more about the role of Hollingsworth in the lives of the two women, he irritates Zenobia into an outburst of scorn:

> "Why do you bring up his name at every turn? . . . You know not what you do! It is dangerous, sir, believe me, to tamper thus with earnest human passions, out of your mere idleness, and for your sport. I will endure it no longer!" (V, 514)

Precisely this curious species of interest bars Coverdale from the confidence of his three friends. As he prepares to leave the farm for his holiday in Boston, Zenobia tells him:

> "Do you know, Mr. Coverdale, that I have been several times on the point of making you my confidant, for lack of a better and wiser one? But you are too young to be my father confessor; and you would not thank me for treating you like one of those good little handmaidens who share the bosom secrets of a tragedy-queen."
>
> "I would, at least, be loyal and faithful," answered I, "and would counsel you with an honest purpose, if not wisely."
>
> "Yes," said Zenobia, "you would be only too wise, too honest. Honesty and wisdom are such a delightful pastime, at another's expense!"
>
> "Ah, Zenobia," I exclaimed, "if you would but let me speak!"
>
> "By no means," she replied, "especially when you have just resumed the whole series of social conventionalism, together with that strait-bodied coat. I would as lief open my heart to a lawyer or to a clergyman!" (V, 482)

A very similar scene takes place, as we shall see, in *The Marble Faun*, when Miriam considers, then rejects, Kenyon as a confidant.

When Coverdale reaches the city he finds that the drama

which has been absorbing him has shifted conveniently to an apartment whose windows face his hotel room. As he stands behind his curtain watching the figures of Westervelt, Zenobia, and Priscilla across the intervening space, he reminds one of his protoype in the sketch "Sunday at Home." He muses:

> ... there seemed something fatal in the coincidence that had borne me to this one spot, of all others in a great city, and transfixed me there, and compelled me again to waste my already wearied sympathies on affairs which were none of mine, and persons who cared little for me. It irritated my nerves; it affected me with a kind of heart-sickness. After the effort which it cost me to fling them off,—after consummating my escape, as I thought, from these goblins of flesh and blood, and pausing to revive myself with a breath or two of an atmosphere in which they should have no share,—it was a positive despair, to find the same figures arraying themselves before me, and presenting their old problem in a shape that made it more insoluble than ever (V, 498-99) .

The fatality of which Coverdale speaks is psychologically nothing but his own compulsion to watch and analyze the lives of others—as Hawthorne felt the artist must. From this obsession, indeed, he cannot escape.

Coverdale soon begins to feel that his detached curiosity is immoral and inhuman, as Hawthorne's artists generally do discover. He admits quite early:

> It is not, I apprehend, a healthy kind of mental occupation, to devote ourselves too exclusively to the study of individual men and women. If the person under examination be one's self, the result is pretty certain to be diseased action of the heart, almost before we can snatch a second glance. Or, if we take the freedom to put a friend under our microscope, we thereby insulate him from many of his true relations, magnify his peculiarities, inevitably tear him into parts, and, of course, patch him together very clumsily again (V, 398) .

As he leaves Blithedale for Boston, he reflects:

> I was full of idle and shapeless regrets. The thought impressed itself upon me that I had left duties unperformed. With the power, perhaps, to act in the place of destinity and avert misfortune from my friends, I had resigned them to their fate. That cold tendency, between instinct and intellect, which made me pry with a speculative interest into people's passions and impulses, appeared to have gone far towards unhumanizing my heart (V, 495).

Zenobia gives Coverdale a still more cutting account of his own character:

> "I have long recognized you as a sort of transcendental Yankee, with all the native propensity of your countrymen to investigate matters that come within their range, but rendered almost poetical, in your case, by the refined methods which you adopt for its gratification" (V, 505).

Coverdale pleads that "an uncertain sense of some duty to perform" brings his mind to dwell upon his friends, but Zenobia hisses derisively,

> "Oh, this stale excuse of duty! ... I have often heard it before from those who sought to interfere with me, and I know precisely what it signifies. Bigotry; self-conceit; an insolent curiosity; a meddlesome temper; a coldblooded criticism, founded on a shallow interpretation of half-perceptions; a monstrous scepticism in regard to any conscience or any wisdom, except one's own; a most irreverent propensity to thrust Providence aside, and substitute one's self in its awful place, —out of these, and other motives as miserable as these, comes your idea of duty! But beware, sir! With all your fancied acuteness, you step blindfold into these affairs. For any mischief that may follow your interference, I hold you responsible!" (V, 514-15)

Coverdale finds himself separated from those who most interest him, "excluded from everybody's confidence, and attaining no further, by my most earnest study, than to an uncertain sense of something hidden from me" (V, 518). He returns sadly to Blithedale.

> Hollingsworth, Zenobia, Priscilla! They glided mistily before me, as I walked. Sometimes, in my solitude, I laughed with the bitterness of self-scorn, remembering how unreservedly I had given up my heart and soul to interests that were not mine. . . . It was both sad and dangerous, I whispered to myself, to be in too close affinity with the passions, the errors, and the misfortunes of individuals who stood within a circle of their own, into which, if I stept at all, it must be as an intruder, and at a peril that I could not estimate (V, 552-53).

Zenobia's last talk with him before her suicide contains the final taunt: "Is it you, Miles Coverdale? . . . Ah, I perceive what you are about! You are turning this whole affair into a ballad. Pray let me hear as many stanzas as you happen to have ready" (V, 572).

The Blithedale Romance includes, then, among its fundamental themes, the bankruptcy of the transcendental artist as a human participant. As Coverdale discovers that the idealism of the Blithedalers does not succeed in its aim of ennobling life—"the clods of earth, which we so constantly belabored and turned over and over, were never etherealized into thought" (V, 394)—he also discovers that the artist's egotism is a fatal deformity which separates him from his brother men. He may not love or be loved. Coverdale's final declaration that he has all along been in love with Priscilla does not carry conviction. In his psychologizing interest in her affairs, his own emotions would seem to have been absorbed. She, in her turn, never thinks of "Mr. Coverdale" as a lover at all. One must admit that Coverdale cuts rather a poor figure in his own tale.

One suspects, really, that he has loved Zenobia. T[...] may be supposed not merely because of the obvious fascination her personality has exercised upon him—he has, after all, also been interested in his other two friends, Hollingsworth and Priscilla. But Zenobia is plainly one of Hawthorne's magnetic ladies of experience, resembling Beatrice Rappaccini even to the flower with which she is associated —a woman beautiful, mysteriously tainted, and fated to death. Thus, as I have noted before, she represents the allure and the penalty of the artist's forbidden knowledge. He would, indeed, save himself by loving the modest Priscilla, the blond young priestess of innocence. Such was the rescue of the Village Uncle, as we have seen, and such will be the redemption of Holgrave and of Kenyon, the artist-heroes of Hawthorne's two later novels. But, with the rather matter-of-fact realism that distinguishes this work above any others by Hawthorne, the story does not permit this recovery to Coverdale. He will go on, one supposes, being that cursed thing, a writer.

The House of the Seven Gables is, we have noted, a story steeped in the variegated symbolism of the Gothic romance, and Holgrave, the artist with the wizard eye, is, to begin with, a symbol of the menacing qualities attributed to the Gothic, Faustian intellectual. His descent from the wizard of colonial times, Matthew Maule, is a deliberate metaphor. Holgrave, like his ancestor, possesses an acuity concerning the inner workings of the soul which seems somehow illicit and dangerous, and which is represented in his skill as a mesmerist. But Holgrave also exists on the realist level suggested by his appearance not under the Maule name, but under a new, ancestorless one. Throughout the novel we are made aware of the double nature of this Maule-Holgrave. As Holgrave, he is a young man of varied though commonplace experience, given to numerous intellectual enthusiasms, who takes portraits by means of the newfangled daguerreotype and writes stories for current magazines—in other words, an American artist of the eighteen-forties. The Maule element acts, as occult material generally does in Hawthorne's work, to bring into the discourse the moral viewpoint of an older tradition in which men were burnt at the stake for witchcraft and in which knowledge that was not moral knowledge was considered the Devil's art.

Some of the Maule characteristics which Holgrave inherits may be considered characterizations of the Romantic-Gothic view of the artist's temperament.

> So long as any of the race were to be found, they had been marked out from other men—not strikingly, nor as with a sharp line, but with an effect that was felt rather than spoken of—by an hereditary character of reserve. Their companions, or those who endeavored to become such, grew conscious of a circle round about the Maules, within the sanctity or the spell of which, in spite of an exterior of sufficient frankness and good-fellowship, it was impossible for any man to step. It was this indefinable peculiarity, perhaps, that, by insulating them from human aid, kept them always so unfortunate in life. It certainly operated to prolong in their case, and to confirm to them as their only inheritance, those feelings of repugnance and superstitious terror with which the people of the town, even after awakening from their frenzy, continued to regard the memory of the reputed witches. The mantle, or rather the ragged cloak, of old Matthew Maule, had fallen upon his children. They were half believed to inherit mysterious attributes; the family eye was said to possess strange power. Among other good-for-nothing properties and privileges, one was especially assigned them—that of exercising an influence over people's dreams (III, 41-42) .

Here we see the traits that are the now quite familiar lineaments of Hawthorne's portrait of the artist. The reserved personality, with its suggestion of an inner fastness inaccessible to others; the penalty of a solitary doom; the impression of mystic attributes and strange power; the ability especially to move the nonrational half of man's nature, the world of dream and imagination—these might as easily have been distinguished in the painter-hero of "The Prophetic Pictures."

Now what has such a somber complex to do with Holgrave, the Yankee jack-of-all-trades, who had been a strolling schoolmaster, a lecturer on mesmerism, a salesman in a village store, a district schoolmaster, the editor of a country newspaper, and who "had subsequently traveled New England and the Middle States as a peddler, in the employment of a Connecticut manufactory of Cologne water and other essences" (III, 212). He is, to begin with, an *artist*— a writer and a daguerreotype portraitist. His name, he tells Phoebe, with some pique at her ignorance of it, "has figured . . . on the covers of Graham and Godey, making as respectable an appearance, for aught I could see, as any of the canonized bead-roll with which it was associated" (III, 223); the story of Alice Pyncheon, which forms Chapter XIII of *The House of the Seven Gables*, is said to be one of his compositions. As a photographer, he has as keen an interest in the disclosure of the secret springs of personality as he already possesses as a story writer. He praises the daguerreotype for its truth-telling power:

> There is a wonderful insight in Heaven's broad and simple sunshine. While we give it credit only for depicting the merest surface, it actually brings out the secret character with a truth that no painter would venture upon, even could he detect it (III, 116).

Consequently his portrait of Judge Pyncheon reveals that smiling hypocrite's inner nature and shows Holgrave to be possessed of the hereditary Maule clairvoyance in the guise of artistic perception.

But, like his forebears, Holgrave is insulated from the flow of human sympathy. Phoebe thinks his hardly an affectionate nature.

> He was too calm and cool an observer. Phoebe felt his eye, often; his heart, seldom or never. He took a certain kind of interest in Hepzibah and her brother, and in Phoebe herself. He studied them attentively, and allowed no slightest circumstances of their individualities to escape him. He was ready to do them whatever good he might; but after all, he never exactly made common cause with them, nor gave any reliable evidence that he loved them better in proportion as he knew them more. In his relations with them, he seemed to be in quest of mental food, not heart-sustenance. Phoebe could not conceive what interested him so much in her friends and herself, intellectually, since he cared nothing for them, or, comparatively, so little, as objects of human affection (III, 213).

As Miles Coverdale was fascinated by the riddle of Hollingsworth, Zenobia, and Priscilla, so Holgrave is drawn by the mystery of the House of the Seven Gables, where he pursues studies, he tells Phoebe, not in books, but of another sort (III, 221). Particularly does the enigmatic history of Clifford Pyncheon intrigue him. "Had I your opportunities," he says to Phoebe another time, "no scruples would prevent me from fathoming Clifford to the full depth of my plummet-line!" (III, 214) She in turn later asks him frankly whether he wishes good or ill to Hepzibah and her brother. He answers:

> "Undoubtedly ... I do feel an interest in this antiquated, poverty-stricken old maiden lady, and this degraded and shattered gentleman, this abortive lover of the beautiful. A kindly interest, too, helpless old children that they are! But you have no conception of what a different kind of heart mine is from your own. It is not my impulse, as regards these two indi-

viduals, either to help or hinder; but to look on, to analyze, to explain matters to myself, and to comprehend the drama which, for almost two hundred years, has been dragging its slow length over the ground where you and I now tread. If permitted to witness the close, I doubt not to derive a moral satisfaction from it, go matters how they may."

But Phoebe protests:

> "I wish you would speak more plainly . . . and above all, that you would feel more like a Christian and a human being! How is it possible to see people in distress, without desiring, more than anything else, to help and comfort them? You talk as if this old house were a theatre; and you seem to look at Hepzibah's and Clifford's misfortunes, and those of generations before them, as a tragedy, such as I have seen acted in the hall of a country hotel, only the present one appears to be played exclusively for your amusement. I do not like this. The play costs the performers too much, and the audience is too cold-hearted" (III, 258-59) .

But the Maule element does not finally prevail in Holgrave's character. He refrains from exercising his mesmerist skill over Phoebe, and appears to give up his intellectual quest, finally, for love of her. Now Phoebe is one of Hawthorne's most charming heroines—simple, natural, unintellectual. She is the very embodiment of Heart. Her presence in the Pyncheon household makes a home of the cold, old mansion and in praise of her quality Hawthorne writes:

> She was real! Holding her hand, you felt something; a tender something; a substance, and a warm one; and so long as you should feel its grasp, soft as it was, you might be certain that your place was good in the whole sympathetic chain of human nature (III, 171).

This sympathetic chain is precisely what Hawthorne's intellectuals are always in danger of letting slip from their grasp. Ethan Brand, it may be recalled, having cultivated his mental powers beyond the eminence of the philosophers of the earth, was said to have "lost his hold of the magnetic chain of humanity" (III, 495). Phoebe places Holgrave's hand upon it again. Her closest cousin in Hawthorne's fiction is probably Susan, in "The Village Uncle," who leads her artist-husband to renounce his obsessions of solitary achievement for "chaste and warm affections, humble wishes, and honest toil for some useful end . . ."

Holgrave's destiny is undoubtedly that of the Village Uncle. It is true that we are not specifically told that he will toss aside pen and camera. But we are made to realize that he will surrender the wilder ideas of his youth concerning the possibility of human perfectibility.

> He would still have faith in man's brightening destiny, and perhaps love him all the better, as he should recognize his helplessness in his own behalf; and the haughty faith, with which he began life, would be well bartered for a far humbler one at its close, in discerning that man's best effort accomplishes a kind of dream, while God is the sole worker of realities (III, 216) .

Phoebe fears that Holgrave will lead her out of her own quiet path, but he assures her that, on the contrary, she will lead him.

> The world owes all its onward impulses to men ill at ease. The happy man inevitably confines himself within ancient limits. I have a presentiment that, hereafter, it will be my lot to set out trees, to make fences,—perhaps, even, in due time, to build a house for another generation,—in a word, to conform myself to laws, and the peaceful practice of society (III, 363) .

Mrs. Hawthorne liked the ending of *The House of the Seven Gables* in which the estranged artist-personality is reconciled to normal, everyday life, the conservative pulse of health, through his marriage to Phoebe. It is certainly a more comfortable ending that that of *The Scarlet Letter*, which seems to have sent her to bed with a headache.[1] But it must be admitted that we are left with the impression that Holgrave will never be quite as interesting a man as he promised to be at our first encounter with him. He has broken his magician's staff.

There are so many art-objects in *The Marble Faun*, so many discussions on matters of aesthetic taste, and so many artists in background and foreground, that one would expect Hawthorne's view of the artist to receive profoundest expression here. This is not quite the case. Yet despite the large amount of adventitious guidebook observation, *The Marble Faun* does contain much valuable material reflecting Hawthorne's view of artistic questions. In previous chapters we have already observed the transcendental aestheticism so prominent in Chapter XV, "An Aesthetic Company," and the abundant use in this novel of symbolically magical works of art. In addition, the story itself concerns the fate of the artist as represented by most of the chief characters.

Like *The Blithedale Romance* and *The House of the Seven Gables*, *The Marble Faun* contains an artist-observer, whose prospects of happiness and relations to the lives of others constitute just such a problem as we have seen confronting Coverdale and Holgrave. Kenyon is a less intricately developed character than these previous examples of the artist's nature, and his choice between the warmth of life and the ideal service of art is of less dramatic importance in the book as a whole. Yet he is worth our close attention as Hawthorne's last portrait of an artist.

The very fact that Kenyon is not presented as an idiosyncratic member of society, but as the representative citizen of an art colony, tends to make his relations with the other characters less difficult. He is a more trusted friend of Miriam, Donatello, and Hilda than is Coverdale of Zenobia, Hollingsworth, and Priscilla. He is actually able to help his friends to solve their problems, and he succeeds in winning happiness himself by winning the love of his Puritan sweetheart, as Coverdale does not. In this he resembles Holgrave, who by gaining Phoebe achieves the norm and all the hearthside joys that belong to it, although to begin with Holgrave's peril is greater than Kenyon's.

Yet Kenyon contains all the traits—indicated less darkly, perhaps—which characterize Hawthorne's artists. It would seem that he himself believes that natural feeling is incompatible with intellectual development, for he explains that Donatello possesses in abundance those emotional qualities which Miriam must find lacking in herself—and which, by implication, Kenyon likewise misses—"the wholesome gush of natural feeling, the honest affection, the simple joy, the fulness of contentment with what he loves. . . . True, she may call him a simpleton. It is a necessity of the case; for a man loses the capacity for this kind of affection, in proportion as he cultivates and refines himself" (VI, 129). At a crucial moment of desperate need, Miriam rejects Kenyon's counsel because she senses some central failure of sympathy in his cool nature. First appealing to him passionately for help, she suddenly draws back.

> "Ah, I shall hate you!" cried she, echoing the thought which he had not spoken; she was half choked with the gush of passion that was thus turned back upon her. "You are as cold and pitiless as your own marble."
>
> "No; but full of sympathy, God knows!" replied he. . . ."
>
> "Keep your sympathy, then, for sorrows that admit of such solace," said she, making a strong effort to compose herself. "As for my griefs, I know how to manage them. It was all a mistake: you can do nothing for me unless you petrify me into

a marble companion for your Cleopatra there ..." (VI, 155-56).

It is interesting to note how closely this conversation parallels the colloquy between Zenobia and Coverdale, previously quoted. But Zenobia rejects Miles Coverdale's interest to the last, jeering at his protestations even as she goes to her death. Miriam, on the other hand, finally accepts the assistance of Kenyon in regaining Donatello's trust, assenting to the plan he formulates by which she is able to meet her unhappy lover by the statue of Pope Julius in Perugia. And eventually both she and Donatello put their problem before this friend.

> "Speak!" said Miriam. "We confide in you."
> "Speak!" said Donatello. "You are true and upright (VI, 368).

Kenyon has the artist's gift of discernment. Piece by piece he puts together the tragic story of Miriam and Donatello's crime before they tell him anything about it. Witnessing the curious attitude of Miriam at the bier of the dead Capuchin, his nerves suddenly signal alarm.

> Kenyon, as befitted the professor of an imaginative art, was endowed with an exceedingly quick sensibility, which was apt to give him intimations of the true state of matters that lay beyond his actual vision. There was a whisper in his ear: it said, "Hush!" (VI, 221)

His intuitive understanding is, of course, illustrated most strongly in his art itself. His bust of Donatello has the same sort of divined truth as Holgrave's daguerreotype of Judge Pyncheon, and is almost as prescient as the "prophetic pictures." It is Kenyon's aim to exhibit his friend's essential nature, his most personal characteristics.

These it was his difficult office to bring out from their depths, and interpret them to all men, showing them what they could not discern for themselves, yet must be compelled to recognize at a glance, on the surface of a block of marble (VI, 312) .

He is unable to accomplish satisfactory results until he surrenders to the nonrational forces of his nature and becomes a "medium."

Hopeless of a good result, Kenyon gave up all preconceptions about the character of his subject and let his hands work uncontrolled with the clay, somewhat as a spiritual medium while holding a pen, yields it to an unseen guidance other than that of her own will. Now and then he fancied that this plan was destined to be the successful one. A skill and insight beyond his consciousness seemed occasionally to take up the task. The mystery, the miracle, of imbuing an inanimate substance with thought, feeling, and all the intangible attributes of the soul, appeared on the verge of being wrought. And now, as he flattered himself, the true image of his friend was about to emerge from the facile material, bringing with it more of Donatello's character than the keenest observer could detect at any one moment in the face of the original (VI, 313) .

This piece of sculpture, as it progresses, is truly a "living" work of art, a magic statue, assuming in succession the representation of Donatello's past and future development as a moral being. Working in exasperated frenzy the sculptor suddenly comes upon the Donatello who had hurled Miriam's persecutor from the Tarpeian Rock:

By some accidental handling of the clay, entirely independent of his own will, Kenyon had given the countenance a distorted and violent look, combining animal fierceness with intelligent hatred. Had Hilda, or had Miriam, seen the bust, with the expression which it had now assumed, they might have recognized Donatello's face as they beheld it at that terrible moment when he held his victim over the edge of the precipice (VI, 314).

The repentant Donatello tells the sculptor to chisel that look in eternal marble, but Kenyon urges that whatever guilt weighs upon his friend's heart can be expiated by good deeds, and changes the expression to one prophetic of the new Donatello.

> They now left the sculptor's temporary studio, without observing that his last accidental touches, with which he hurriedly effaced the look of deadly rage, had given the bust a higher and sweeter expression that it had hitherto worn—for here were still the features of the antique Faun, but now illuminated with a higher meaning, such as the old marble never bore (VI, 315-16).

The "transformation," to which Hawthorne's English title for the book referred, has taken place. The Faun of Praxiteles has come alive in the living man and in the "living" statue of Kenyon. When, much later, Hilda sees the bust, she remarks on its resemblance to the faun, and says of the new quality of its expression that

> "It has an effect as if I could see this countenance gradually brightening while I look at it. It gives the impression of a growing intellectual power and moral sense. Donatello's face used to evince little more than a genial, pleasurable sort of vivacity, and capability of enjoyment. But, here, a soul is being breathed into him; it is the Faun, but advancing towards a state of higher development" (VI, 433).

But to Kenyon the desires of the heart prove stronger than even the wonder-working power of art. When Hilda suddenly disappears from Rome he realizes his need of her, and his mind can contain no other interest. Not even the ageless beauty of an ancient statue which Donatello has unearthed can move him now. "Ah Miriam," he exclaims impatiently, "I cannot respond to you. . . . Imagination and the love of art have both died out of me" (VI, 483).

"So Kenyon won the gentle Hilda's shy affection, and her consent to be his bride" (VI, 520-21). With this fairy-tale consummation ends the story of Hawthorne's artist. "The mind wanders wild and wide," Kenyon declares, "and so lonely as I live and work, I have neither pole-star above nor light of cottage-windows here below to bring me home. Were you my guide, my counsellor, my inmost friend, with that white wisdom which clothes you as a celestial garment, all would go well. O Hilda, guide me home" (VI, 520). Despite her unearthly purity, we suspect that Hilda is doing the office of Susan of Swampscott for the Village Uncle. Kenyon's children, one imagines, will be cautioned not to whittle woodshavings, lest they fall into perilous ways.

Perhaps we should here add a word about Hawthorne's artist-heroines in two of the novels—Zenobia, the writer, in *The Blithedale Romance,* and Miriam, the painter, in *The Marble Faun.* Strangely similar, these two women are the most tragically blighted of all Hawthorne's dark heroines, less vernal than Beatrice Rappaccini, less triumphant in expiation than Hester Prynne. All four women, of course, are intellectuals—Hester becomes an audacious thinker and Beatrice is reputed to have absorbed her father's learning along with the poison that has infiltrated her system. But Zenobia and Miriam are, like Coverdale and Kenyon, the men who observe them, dedicated to the perilous service of art itself. And art has somehow made them unhappy, distorted their feminity, as Hawthorne understood the quality, and doomed one, at least, to tragic death. I say "art" had done this—but, of course, Hawthorne really suggests that some unspecified experience, some moral taint, had already touched and altered Zenobia and Miriam before we meet them in the stories. Only in the case of Hester has he clearly explained his dark heroine's sins as somehow sexual; for the others we have only vague hints. And in the case of his artist-heroines, it is possible that the aim and life of art bear a direct relationship to sin. Just as Zenobia and Miriam symbolize the dark marriage with experience which is offered to the artist who is a man, so, in themselves, they are also examples of the penalty of the life of art.

Of Zenobia's activities as a writer, we see and hear little, though indeed we see more of her art than we do of Coverdale's, for the inset-story of Chapter XIII, "The Silvery Veil," is a narrative extemporized by her before an audience of Blithedalers. But we get a much more detailed picture of Miriam's performances as an artist, and, indeed, her works of art have a symbolic function to play in the narrative. Miriam's studio, the habitation of a character who is both artist and "dark lady" of experience, is the shadowy source of art-objects obscurely and dangerously prophetic. When Donatello visits her she tells him: "We artists purposely exclude sunshine, and all but a partial light, because we think it necessary to put ourselves at odds with Nature before trying to imitate her" (VI, 57). She thus identifies herself for us as an artist whose sources of power are darker and more hidden than those present in the sunny workshop of the woodcarver Drowne. Donatello is alarmed by a glimpse of a wooden lay figure, who appeared to be "a woman with long dark hair, who threw up her arms with a wild gesture of tragic despair" (VI, 58), and though reassured that she is only a pliable mannikin (or that, symbolically, the artist's imagination is the obedient subject of his will) he is shaken by the impression that "her arms moved, as if beckoning me to help her in some direful peril" —a clear prophecy, we know, of a scene of crime that he and Miriam will soon enact. And insistently prophetic as well are the artist's own sketches—one of Jael, driving the nail through the temple of Sisera, which seemed to Donatello to have the force of a "bloody confession" (VI, 60), another of Judith with the head of Holofernes"—"over and over again . . . the idea of woman, acting the part of a re-vengeful mischief towards man" (VI, 61). Of these, she herself confesses an unwilled origin: "They are ugly things that stole out of my mind; not things that I created, but things that haunt me" (VI, 61).

Surely this is a mischief-making art—not only prophetic but actually suggestive to the beholder—and arising from an uncanny and plainly unheavenly source. It does not surprise us, even without the extra moral mystery to scent out in Miriam's background, that she suffers the lonely estrangement of the artist of the "prophetic pictures." During the visit just described, she shows Donatello other products of her pencil and brush: sketches and paintings of such themes as a maiden's first love, an infant's first shoe, and so on. But always she had included in these scenes of homely happiness a melancholy, watching figure curiously resembling herself. It would seem to be Miriam's acknowl-edgment that from such happy scenes she was forever ex-cluded.

What love, the love of Donatello, will do to Miriam's art after the long period of penance is past Hawthorne does not tell us. In the face of the greater moral mystery of the transformed faun and his destiny, Hawthorne has lost in-terest in Miriam's vocation as an artist. But her character and her story as we do see it already suggest the reason why, like Kenyon, she too falls in love with a simple and un-corrupt soul who feels no need to rival divine creation with his wits. It is quite understandable that the pure Hilda is not really an artist but a copyist of rare skill, wonderfully sympathetic and wonderfully adept at catching the life of art created at such cost by darker spirits.

NOTE TO CHAPTER VII

[1] Stewart, *Nathaniel Hawthorne*, pp. 113, 95.

Chapter VIII

"Refractions of the Artistic Nature":

Fanshawe, Aylmer, Clifford, Ilbrahim

In Hawthorne's various studies of the artist we have seen what he considered to be the consequences of absorption in an ideal goal, of a peculiar ability to see the truths of human personality and destiny, and of the necessity for personal indifference to humane considerations. Now we shall note how these characteristics appear also in the careers of a large number of the nonartist personalities in Hawthorne's stories.

Absorption in an ideal goal to the detriment of social obligations is the path chosen by the "scholar-idealists," as Stewart calls them—that parade which begins with Fanshawe, the studious melancholy youth, and ends with Septimius Felton, the strangely similar zealot of science whose story occupied Hawthorne's mind more than thirty years later. In this company are included such personages as Aylmer, the aesthetic scientist obsessed with the idea of perfect beauty, and even, perhaps, the terrible Dr. Rappaccini, with his "spiritual love of science." Having some emotional affinity to them are those for whom a social or religious, rather than an aesthetic or scientific, perfection is the goal of all striving—the Quakers of "The Gentle Boy," or the reformer Hollingsworth in *The Blithedale Romance*. The idealistic, the positive Romantic approach was in full tide in all domains of life as Hawthorne wrote. The scientist and the social and religious reformer joined the Romantic poet in a belief in man's power to achieve perfectibility and in man's right to trust, as Emerson advised, in the infinitude of his own mind. The idealist identity of truth and beauty merged the aims of the artist, the moralist, and the seeker after Nature's ultimate secrets; in examining the last two figures, Hawthorne spoke to the problem of the artist also.[1]

In the perfectionism of the political and social reformer Hawthorne saw a dangerous self-delusion, as he clearly showed in "Earth's Holocaust," that fantasy in which mankind attempts to throw upon a bonfire all the world's "wornout trumpery." Left unconsumed and unpurified is the foul human heart—the source from which all the rest would issue again, as the dark-visaged stranger points out to the narrator, who muses: "How sad a truth, if true it were, that man's agelong endeavor for perfection had served only to render him the mockery of the evil principle, from the fatal circumstance of an error at the very root of the matter!" (II, 455) Indeed, Hawthorne went further and found that, no less than other forms of perfectionism, the reformer's was egotistical presumption and led to obliteration of the capacity to love God and one's fellow man. Hollingsworth's destructive career seems to Coverdale to be an illustration of the fact that the most philanthropic of ruling passions is a moral danger. He found it "an exemplification of the most awful truth in Bunyan's book of such—that from the very gate of heaven there is a by-way to the pit!" (V, 595)

That it is their perfectionist idealism that links together such "scientific" seekers as Rappaccini and Aylmer, though one is revolting in his inhumane mania and the other almost admirable, is apparent when we recall that Hawthorne's scientists are not empirical investigators of natural events, but Faustian necromancers who aspire to disclose the ultimate mysteries of the universe. No more than Owen Warland are they interested in "the perpetual motion." According to this looser use of the title "scientist," the artist Warland is, indeed, another experimenter in the tradition, as he himself indicates, of Albertus Magnus and his fabulous Man of Brass, or Friar Bacon and his Brazen Head (II, 524) rather than in the tradition of the arts; his effort to construct a living mechanical butterfly might have been one of the projects undertaken by Aylmer. In this sense, such a story as "The Great Carbuncle" is highly significant for us, not merely because it contains a portrait of a transcendental poet, but because included in his company are other "seekers" similarly deluded—a dreamer, a scientist, a lord mad with hereditary pride, and a merchant obsessed by his pile of shillings. All alike, Hawthorne seems to say, are dupes of the Romantic quest for the absolute, of which, indeed, the story is a sort of parody, a satiric *Heinrich von Ofterdingen*.

As "The Prophetic Pictures" indicates, Hawthorne often felt that the artist's vision, which enabled him to "see into the heart of things" and into the inner thoughts of men, was more sinister than divine. He distrusted the habit of observation, and during his daughter Una's babyhood he felt a repugnance toward recording the events of her innocent days, "not because there is not much to record, but because I seem to comprehend and feel it better while it remains unwritten. It would be dangerous to meddle with it."[2] As we have seen in the preceding chapters, the danger is symbolically represented in "The Prophetic Pictures," but shown more realistically in Hawthorne's other studies of the artist who must dissect dispassionately to learn the workings of the human soul, yet can share none of the passions he observes. This is what Zenobia accuses Miles Coverdale of doing, and the same cold interest is attributed to the sculptor Kenyon by Miriam in a strikingly similar scene. A like charge might have been made against Holgrave by Phoebe, who "had felt his eye, often; his heart, seldom or never" (III, 213). Now Ethan Brand, who in his study of the human soul "converted men and women to be puppets," is not unrelated to these characters. A passage in the *American Notebooks* which seems to be the germ of "Ethan Brand" clearly reveals the nature of the "unpardonable sin" of which lonely Brand is self-convicted:

> The unpardonable sin might consist in a want of love and reverence for the Human Soul; in consequence of which, the investigator pried into its dark depths, not with a hope or purpose of making it better, but from cold philosophical curiosity,—content that it should be wicked in whatever kind or degree, and only desiring to study it out.[3]

This, almost exactly, is the fault of the painter of the prophetic pictures: "He had pried into their souls with his keenest insight," revealing the fearful darkness in the natures of his two subjects, yet "his heart was cold . . ." (I, 206). But it is also the crime of nonartists like Brand and Chillingworth, remote as they are from the innocuous Miles Coverdale, that they employ for evil ends an abnormally developed skill in the dissection of the soul.

Some of Hawthorne's worst villains, it has already been remarked, are men endowed with peculiar powers to read the hearts of others and to control them. Chillingworth, skilled in the intimate delving of the physician, makes use of his abilities to gain access to Dimmesdale's secret. The vaguely horrible Westervelt, like the wizard Maule, and probably Brand, possesses the penetrative power of the mesmerist. As I have pointed out earlier, it is highly significant that Holgrave, the artist, not only possesses these mesmeric powers himself, but is a lineal descendent of Matthew Maule, with his occult wizard eye. The "second sight" of the artist here exists on a double plane—both as the faculty developed by his vocation and as something else, an endowment transmitted to him as the necromancer's hell-purchased art. In his status as both a Maule and an artist (under, we note, a pseudonym), Holgrave links Hawthorne's artist-figures with the diabolic set of characters who misuse their psychological knowledge.

The gift of insight was often regarded by Hawthorne as the fruit of that morbid self-absorption that he considered typical of the artistic nature. Years of lonely introspection were, we know, his own prelude to professional recognition, and he sometimes felt, as the familiar letters to Longfellow and Sophia Peabody show, that this immuring had entailed deep spiritual hazard.[4] Roderick Elliston, the afflicted hero of "Egotism; or the Bosom Serpent," may have been intended as another of Hawthorne's artist-portraits, for he is presented as a writer of stories, the narrator of "The Christmas Banquet," also in *Mosses from an Old Manse.* Cursed because he could not forget himself, the "once brilliant young man . . . prided and gloried himself on being marked out from the ordinary experiences of mankind by the possession of a double nature, and a life within a life" by which he derived an insight into other bosoms. Secret sin, which resembles the artist's egotistical self-absorption, is the means by which other Hawthorne characters gain an illicit informedness about the sins of others. Thus the Reverend Mr. Dimmesdale finds himself suddenly possessed of such powers as he returns from his interview with Hester in the forest. Such, too, is the vision of Young Goodman Brown, after he has partaken of the Devil's sacrament.

One can probably distinguish still other traits of the artistic character which are matched in Hawthorne's non-artist characters. The wayward surrender to his bent by which, as Hawthorne himself experienced it, the artist seems to be drawn away from the hearth of natural affections is, as we have seen, the experience of Oberon, who declares of his literary manuscripts:

> They have drawn me aside from the beaten path of the world, and let me into a strange sort of solitude,—a solitude of men —where nobody wishes for what I do, nor thinks nor feels as I do. The tales have done all this (III, 576).

But it is also the tragedy of Wakefield. Not that he is any sort of creative genius:

> He was intellectual, but not actively so; his mind occupied itself in long and lazy musings, that ended to no purpose, or had no vigor to attain it; his thoughts were seldom so energetic as to seize hold of words. Imagination, in the proper meaning of the term, made no part of Wakefield's gifts (I, 154).

Hawthorne denies almost too firmly that Wakefield is an artist; we sense the implication that *therefore* does his strange desertion of his wife seem most paradoxical. This, Hawthorne intimates, is the sort of action expected rather of a man "feverish with riotous thoughts ... perplexed with originality." But "Wakefield" is a symbolic story. He who by stepping aside for a moment "exposes himself to a fearful risk of losing his place forever" (I, 164), for whom the moral which concludes the story is meant, may well be the artist who, like Wakefield, finds that he has lived half his life away a stranger to his own kin, though he had but to stretch out a hand to reach them.

Hawthorne felt that the sensual side of the artist's nature represented a particular weakness inherent in his delicately organized personality. As he says, in explaining the surrender of poor Owen Warland to the pleasures of the tavern: "When the ethereal portion of a man of genius is obscured, the earthly part assumes an influence the more uncontrollable" (II, 519). In Clifford the parallel surrender is to simple appetite for food.

I have tried to suggest by means of this summary of parallels that when Hawthorne sketched his other, nonartist characters, he was often thinking primarily of the artist, as well as that his artists are meant to represent general human qualities. Taken together, these portraits of artists and artists-in-disguise give a full picture of Hawthorne's view of the artistic personality. It cannot be maintained, however, that Hawthorne was writing deliberate allegories of the artist's life in the instances of nonartist behavior which have just been glanced at. Like all great writers he was interested in human problems; even his studies of artists are, ultimately, only examples of his convictions concerning sin and redemption, tragedy and happiness. To Hawthorne, the artist was only another man, susceptible to certain temptations and a certain fate common to many men.

Stewart has called the "scholar-idealist" "the most important single type of character in Hawthorne's work."[5] A recognizable kinship exists between Fanshawe, the hero of Hawthorne's first novel, the scientist Aylmer in "The Birthmark," Dimmesdale, the Puritan minister in *The Scarlet Letter,* that "abortive lover of the beautiful," Clifford Pyncheon in *The House of the Seven Gables,* and Owen Warland, the true artist. The connection is more than one of accidental similarity of physical description. In all these character studies, Hawthorne was concerned with essentially the same question. Is not the obsessive quest for truth or beauty possibly dehumanizing, even sinful, since apparently it leads to an atrophy of the functions of affection and social responsibility? Hawthorne's great European contemporary, Balzac, simultaneously expressed a similar thought in his story, "The Quest of the Absolute," published in 1834, which shows the destructive results of a

man's devotion to the search for the philosopher's stone—
a search that, although idealistic rather than mercenary, yet
makes an inhuman monster of a once affectionate human
being.

Fanshawe is probably far more important for the study of
this fundamental preoccupation than it has been customary
to suppose. Although this early novel obviously had its inspiration in Gothic models, it represents, as Carl Bode has
pointed out, Hawthorne's earliest announcement of a most
personal theme: the justification of the artist's way of life.[6]
In portraying the scholar Fanshawe, Hawthorne may have
considered the outcome of the course upon which he had
already embarked, and asked himself "to what purpose
was all his destructive labor, and where was the happiness
of superior knowledge?" (XI, 93) *Fanshawe* is Hawthorne's
Lycidas.

It may be objected that while Fanshawe is never specifi-
cally described as an artist of any sort, two of the other
principal characters in the book are poets—Hugh Crombie,
the tavern versifier, and Fanshawe's friend and rival Edward
Walcott, the Class Poet of Harley College. However, we
have here an early illustration of the fact that Hawthorne's
artist-representatives are frequently nonartists, for Fanshawe, and not Hugh Crombie or Edward Walcott, displays
the life-problem of the artist in this story.

Fanshawe is the first in Hawthorne's line of exceptional
individuals, a man whose expression "was proud and high,
perhaps triumphant, like one who was a ruler in a world of
his own, and independent of the beings that surround him"
(XI, 88). Like Hawthorne himself, during the early years
after college, he leads a solitary life, committed to his study
table save for a lonely walk at sunset. He is "a solitary
being . . . unconnected with the world, unconcerned in its
feelings, and uninfluenced by it in any of his pursuits" (XI,
93), who gives his life to researches that have no apparent
human purpose.

Hawthorne writes that Fanshawe resembled Nathaniel Mather "in his almost insane eagerness for knowledge and in his early death" (XI, 217). More important than the doom of early death is the doom of renunciation. He loves but renounces Ellen Langton, the "eternal womanly," the joy-giving partner of an average life.

> He had read her character with accuracy, and had seen how fit she was to love, and to be loved, by a man who could find happiness in the common occupations of the world; and Fanshawe never deceived himself so far as to suppose that this would be the case with him (XI, 199).

His love for her was "the yearning of a soul, formed by Nature in a peculiar mould for communion with those to whom it bore a resemblance yet of whom it was not" (XI, 199-200). Ellen, in her turn, really loves the entirely normal man Edward Walcott. It is he who can accept without regret the mediocrity which Fanshawe casts aside.

> Ellen's gentle, almost imperceptible, but powerful influence, drew her husband away from the passions and pursuits that would have interfered with domestic felicity; and he never regretted the worldly distinction of which she thus deprived him (XI, 218) .

Fanshawe's history is the perfect pattern of the Romantic type of unhappy poet. It resembles, for example, the actual career of the poet Henry Kirk White, who worked himself into consumption while a Cambridge student, and who died, in 1806, at twenty-one.[7] *Fanshawe* thus states a theme which will recur in Hawthorne's work until the very end: art (or the scholar's arduous devotion) is an isolating occupation, which destroys the capacity for normal happiness. Hawthorne does not idealize Fanshawe's isolation or give it any sulphurous splendor, such as is manifested in the careers of Byron's heroes, but coldly regards what seems to him to be the inevitable consequence and cost of genius. Those who would be happy should not make Fanshawe's choice, nor, as we have seen, the choice of Owen Warland. Rather, like the artist Holgrave in *The House of the Seven Gables,* or Kenyon in *The Marble Faun,* or the Village Uncle, that man will be happy, Hawthorne thought, who clasps his simple Ellen, or Annie, or Phoebe, or Hilda, or Susan, with the knowledge that earthly satisfaction is not the reward of the artist's lonely striving. Edward Walcott, the Class Poet —we must remember—knows this when he resigns the dedicated life of art, and his marriage with Ellen is one of "calm and quiet bliss." And, Hawthorne asks, "what matters it, that except in these pages, they have left no name behind them?" (XI, 218)

The attempt to combine human happiness with the service of the ideal fails tragically in the story "The Birthmark." Aylmer, though cast as a Gothic scientist, may be viewed as another "Artist of the Beautiful." He strives to reach the realm of absolute beauty by creating it in the person of his wife, whose tiny imperfection is "the fatal flaw of humanity which Nature, in one shape or another, stamps ineffaceably on all her productions, either to imply that they are temporary and finite, or that their perfection must be wrought by toil and pain" (II, 50). Aylmer's aim is that of the artist Pygmalion, to whom he compares himself as he declares to Georgiana, "What will be my triumph when I shall have corrected what Nature left imperfect in her fairest work! Even Pygmalion, when his sculptured woman assumed life, felt no greater ecstacy than mine will be" (II, 53). But as he creates this beauty the human life of his wife gradually expires, just as in Poe's "The Oval Portrait" the model for the artist's painting passes away as the painting reaches completion.

It seems clear to me that Hawthorne intends Aylmer to represent not merely the idealist genius generally, but the Romantic artist in particular. In describing the "journal" (one is reminded of Hawthorne's own) which Aylmer has kept of his past experiments, Hawthorne seems to be expressing the transcendental view of art which we have encountered elsewhere in his writings. Moreover, the terms of the description apply particularly to the efforts of a literary artist.

The book, in truth, was both the history and emblem of his ardent, ambitious, imaginative, yet practical and laborious life. He handled physical details as if there were nothing beyond them; yet spiritualized them all, and redeemed himself from materialism by his strong and eager aspiration towards the infinite. In his grasp the veriest clod of earth assumed a soul. Georgiana, as she read, reverenced Aylmer and loved him more profoundly than ever, but with a less entire dependence on his judgment than heretofore. Much as he had accomplished, she could not but observe that his most splendid successes were almost invariably failures, if compared with the ideal at which he aimed. His brightest diamonds were the merest pebbles, and felt to be so by himself, in comparison with the inestimable gems which lay hidden beyond his reach. The volume, rich with achievements that had won renown for its author, was yet as melancholy a record as ever mortal hand had penned. It was the sad confession and continual exemplification of the shortcomings of the composite man, the spirit burdened with clay and working in matter, and of the despair that assails the higher nature at finding itself so miserably thwarted by the earthly part. Perhaps every man of genius in whatever sphere might recognize the image of his own experience in Aylmer's journal (II, 61-62).

Aylmer is a Romantic and a transcendentalist, tragically confident that evil, the mark of man's imperfection, can be

eradicated, as the idealist of Hawthorne's day was confident
that moral imperfection could be abolished by means of the
proper social reforms. In his optimistic pursuit of truth
Aylmer has "studied the wonders of the human frame, and
attempted to fathom the very process by which Nature
assimilates all her precious influences from earth and air,
and from the spiritual world, to create and foster man, her
masterpiece," realizing unwillingly that "our great creative
mother, while she amuses us by apparently working in the
broadest sunshine, is yet severely careful to keep her own
secrets, and, in spite of her pretended openness, shows nothing but result" (II, 54). Undeterred by this knowledge,
Aylmer proposes to remove the only mark of material imperfection from the cheek of his wife. Hawthorne, with his
powerful Christian sense of the inextricable mixture of
evil in the human compound, regards Aylmer as a dangerous perfectibilitarian. His attempt is doomed, for "thus
ever, does the gross fatality of earth exult in its invariable
triumph over the immortal essence which, in this sphere
of half-development, demands the completeness of a high
state" (II, 69).

"The Birthmark," as Floyd Stovall has observed, illus-
trates Hawthorne's conception "of the limitations which
the laws of matters impose upon the powers of the mind."[8]
But, as Austin Warren points out,[9] the story concludes with
an ambiguity, for Georgiana tells her husband as she dies:
"You have aimed loftily; you have done nobly. Do not re-
pent that with so high and pure a feeling, you have rejected
the best the earth could offer" (II, 69). Here as clearly as
anywhere in Hawthorne's work we can regard his struggle
with the Romanticism of which he himself was so much a
part. As a novelist obliged to depict life as found, he de-
tected an artistic hazard in the yearning for a superior ideal
of absolute beauty. It is this which may have caused him
to keep in his notebooks so faithful a record of direct ob-

servation and experience. But he went further, seeing perhaps in the Romantic disdain for the actual, involving as it does an overweening arrogance on the part of the artist, and a contempt for the common condition of men, a general human hazard to which the nineteenth-century mind was particularly prone. In terms of an older Christian morality, Hawthorne thought such an attitude even impious, for man, though made in God's image, is blemished by his fall from perfect harmony with God. To ignore the sentence of mortality and original sin is to deem man *still* brother to the angels.

"The Birthmark" is a more terrible "Artist of the Beautiful," for in this story the price of the artist's success is not alone alienation, but the criminal destruction of another human being. Aylmer, unlike Owen Warland, has attempted to combine his impersonal idealism with a human affection, and realizes too late how immiscible are the two.

Holgrave, we will recall, identifies Clifford Pyncheon as an "abortive lover of the beautiful" (III, 258). Clifford, then, represents another aspect of the artist's character—the aesthetic sensibility with all its susceptibility to damage from material life—while Holgrave, as we have seen, displays the dangerous egotism of the solitary artist. Hawthorne was aware of the weaknesses in both halves of the artistic nature; he exhibited the first more particularly in Owen Warland, who, as we shall see, is closely related to Clifford; the weakness of the second half is shown in the painter of "The Prophetic Pictures," who bears some resemblance to Holgrave.

Clifford, unlike the prophetic painter, is victim rather than victimizer. Hawthorne made him a representation of the purely aesthetic temperament crushed and exploited by the materialism represented by Judge Pyncheon. In this enemy, as in other ways, he is like Owen Warland; in fact,

Owen's chief antagonist, Peter Hovenden, is the precursor of Clifford's persecutor.[10] No other characters in Hawthorne's fiction so closely resemble one another as these beings of cold sagacity, unillumined understanding, and materialism. Upon both Owen and Clifford the effect of their personalities is withering.

Clifford's love of beauty might under favoring circumstances have made him an artist. But, thwarted and warped by his long imprisonment, his delicate nature shows itself incapable of tragic fortitude or resolute emotion. It lacks the moral quality to make these possible. As a young man his love of the beautiful had promised much:

> In a character where it should exist as the chief attribute, it would bestow on its possessor an exquisite taste, and an enviable susceptibility of happiness. Beauty would be his life; his aspirations would all tend toward it; and, allowing his frame and physical organs to be in consonance, his own developments would likewise be beautiful. Such a man should have nothing to do with sorrow; nothing with strife; nothing with the martyrdom which, in an infinite variety of shapes, awaits those who have the heart, and will, and conscience, to fight a battle with the world (III, 134).

All this could have been seen at the start of Clifford's career in the Malbone miniature of the young Clifford which is still treasured by his sister Hepzibah. The miniature is another of those prophetic portraits which fascinated Hawthorne as symbols of the artist's ability to see the hidden truth of human character. Clifford's nature was originally gentle, contemplative, delicate, as the picture showed. "He ought never to suffer anything" (III, 98), murmurs Phoebe as she gazes at it. But since he does suffer, these qualities, which would have made him certainly a connoisseur of the arts, if not an artist, survive only as sensuality. He cannot bear to look upon his devoted sister because of her horrid scowl and homely mien. A nature of his sort, says Haw-thorne, "is always selfish in its essence."

> Not to speak it harshly or scornfully, it seemed Clifford's nature to be a Sybarite. It was perceptible, even there, in the dark old parlor, in the inevitable polarity with which his eyes were attracted towards the quivering play of sunbeams through the shadow foliage. It was seen in his appreciating notice of the vase of flowers, the scent of which he inhaled with a zest almost peculiar to a physical organization so re-fined that spiritual ingredients are moulded in with it. It was betrayed in the unconscious smile with which he regarded Phoebe, whose fresh and maidenly figure was both sunshine and flowers,—their essence, in a prettier and more agreeable mode of manifestation. Not less evident was this love and necessity for the Beautiful, in the instinctive caution with which, even so soon, his eyes turned away from his hostess, and wandered to any quarter rather than come back. It was Hepzibah's misfortune,—not Clifford's fault. How could he, —so yellow as she was, so wrinkled, so sad of mien, with that odd uncouthness of a turban on her head, and that most perverse of scowls contorting her brow,—how could he love to gaze at her? But, did he owe her no affection for so much as she had silently given? He owed her nothing. A nature like Clifford's can contract no debts of that kind. It is—we say it without censure, nor in diminution of the claim which it indefeasibly possesses on beings of another mould—it is al-ways selfish in its essence . . . (III, 135-136) .

It is Hawthorne's judgment that such a person lacks the ingredient of heart; had his aesthetic gifts been allowed to flower, the result might not have been moral improvement at all—he might have become a cold devotee of beauty to whom human obligations were secondary:

> . . . an individual of his temper can always be pricked more acutely through his sense of the beautiful and harmonious

than through his heart. It is even possible—for similar cases
have often happened—that if Clifford in his foregoing life,
had enjoyed the means of cultivating his taste to its utmost
perfectibility, that subtile attribute might, before this period,
have completely eaten out or filed away his affections. Shall
we venture to pronounce, therefore, that his long and black
calamity may not have had a redeeming drop of mercy at the
bottom? (III, 139-40)

It can readily be seen that Clifford's nature is much like
that of the Artist of the Beautiful, who is perhaps merely
a Clifford who has survived his battle with the coarseness
of his surroundings. In describing Clifford, Hawthorne has
developed the criticism of the aesthetic nature which is
implicit in the short story. Such a nature is selfish; in it the
subtile attribute of taste takes the place of the attributes of
affection.

The parallel between Owen and Clifford is seen still
more clearly when it is recalled that, for a brief period,
Owen does become a sort of Clifford. When Annie Hovenden proves herself unfit to understand his secret aim, Owen
abandons himself to riot and wine, for, Hawthorne says,
"when the ethereal portion of a man of genius is obscured,
the earthly part assumes an influence the more uncontrollable, because the character is now thrown off the balance
to which Providence has so nicely adjusted it . . ." (II, 519).
The broken Clifford at his sister's dainty breakfast table is
also the aesthetic personality reduced to the level of sensuality—in his case, gluttony takes the place of Owen's sub-
jection to wine. Phoebe notices a look come over his refined
features,

one that had the effect of coarseness on the fine mould and
outline of his countenance, because there was nothing intellectual to temper it. It was a look of appetite. He ate food
with what might almost be termed voracity; and seemed to

forget himself, Hepzibah, the young girl, and everything else around him, in the sensual enjoyment which the bountifully spread table afforded. In his natural system, though high-wrought and delicately refined, a sensibility to the delights of the palate was probably inherent. It would have been kept in check, however, and even converted into an accomplishment, and one of the thousand modes of intellectual culture, had his more ethereal characteristics retained their vigor (III, 133).

It is the shrewd guess of Goethe's Mephistopheles that Faust's striving for the unattainable makes him vulnerable to despair and to the temptations of a life of sensual pleasure. And Wordsworth defended the excesses of Burns by arguing that the temperament of genius inclines a man to pleasure and "is not incompatible with vice [which] leads to misery—the more acute from the sensibilities which are the elements of genius."[11]

Hawthorne believed, as we have seen, that at the heart of the aesthetic nature was a spirit that blighted the normal impulses of affection. Even if this central coldness does not make a man like Clifford actually exploitive of others—he does not run the moral risks of Holgrave, as I have said—his own coldness and the world's coarseness together doom him to isolation. Melville, who felt that the portrait of Hawthorne's Clifford was "full of an awful truth throughout,"[12] found one of the most touching scenes in the book to be that in which Clifford, prompted by a longing to get back into life's full-coursing stream, tries to leap from his balcony to the street below. But he cannot join the throng; his long incarceration has made it impossible for him to regain a place in the parade he left so long ago. In his involuntary severance from other lives Clifford has much in common with all those heroes of Hawthorne's fiction who —willing or not—find themselves cut off from the joys as well as the sorrows of average humanity. Hawthorne writes, indeed, that

> Clifford saw, it may be in the mirror of his deeper conscious-
> ness, that he was an example and representative of that great
> class of people whom an inexplicable Providence is continu-
> ally putting at cross-purposes with the world; breaking what
> seems its own promise in their nature; withholding their
> proper food, and setting poison before them for a banquet;
> and thus—when it might so easily, as one would think, have
> been adjusted otherwise—making their existence a strange-
> ness, a solitude, and torment (III, 181).

Something very personal to Hawthorne has been voiced here, one feels—the artist's sense of exile, which we have found so omnipresent in his writing.

The House of the Seven Gables has, of course, a fairy-tale ending. The bad Judge is dead and Hepzibah and Clifford inherit a fortune, Holgrave marries Phoebe, and the ruined lover of the Beautiful recovers enough of his character "to display some outline of the marvellous grace that was abor-tive in it" (III, 371). Both halves of the artistic nature, Holgrave's and Clifford's, have gently reconciled themselves to life as it may be lived in humble trust and modest affec-tion. It is, as I have said, the ending of a fairy tale, and it conveys no serious promise of hope for the artist.

The penalty of difference appears in many forms in Haw-thorne's writings. Idealist genius appears to be but another of those isolating factors, like secret guilt, or bigotry, or egotism, which sever the individual from mankind. And nearly *all* of Hawthorne's characters are exceptional in some way. There is more than analogy between Hawthorne's preoccupation with this theme of the exceptional man and his view of the artist. It is with particular identification of the fate of the former with the artist's doom that he takes up his various cases of those who by choice or accident are, like the Wandering Jew, "cut off from natural sympathies and blasted with a doom . . . inflicted on no other human being" (II, 558).

Among these "isolatoes," as Melville would have called them, particular interest attaches to the story of Ilbrahim, the Quaker child in "The Gentle Boy." Here, as in *Fanshawe,* we have another illustration of the theme that the service of an ideal—or an art—may isolate and punish, for isolation and death are the destiny of the Quakers who appear in the tale.

The story of "The Gentle Boy," though taking place in 1656, is closely related to the intellectual problems of 1830. Quakerism, with its reliance upon the "inner light," provides a certain parallel with the Romantic surrender to impulse, the faith in personal inspiration that was the ethical and artistic creed of transcendentalism. Writing of the Quakers of the Bay Colony, Hawthorne observes that "the command of the spirit, inaudible except to the soul, and not to be controverted on grounds of human wisdom, was made a plea for most indecorous exhibitions which abstractedly considered, well deserved the moderate chastisement of the rod" (I, 86). One cannot help supposing that Hawthorne had, at least partly, the problem of art in mind when he described the harangue of Ilbrahim's mother as "giving evidence of an imagination hopelessly entangled with her reason" (I, 99). She delivers, in a fever of inspiration, not a heaven-born revelation of truth, but

a vague and incomprehensible rhapsody, which, however, seemed to spread its own atmosphere round the hearer's soul, and to move his feelings by some influence unconnected with the words. As she proceeded, beautiful but shadowy images would sometimes be seen, like bright things moving in a turbid river; or a strong and singularly-shaped idea leaped forth, and seized at once on the understanding of the heart. But the course of her unearthly eloquence soon led her to the persecution of her sect, and from thence the step was short to her peculiar sorrows. She was naturally a woman of mighty passions, and hatred and revenge now wrapped themselves in the garb of piety; the character of her speech was changed, her images became distinct though wild, and her denunciations had an almost hellish bitterness (I, 99-100).

In contrast with misguided "inspiration," we are shown the character of Ilbrahim's foster mother, the tolerant and gentle Dorothy Pearson, whose face was "like a verse of fireside poetry." If anyone might bring this changeling child of wild inspiration, "the little wanderer from a remote and heathen country" (I, 107), into happy relation with ordinary life, it is Dorothy, the muse of a domesticated and humble art. But the foster mother cannot protect the child, whose true mother is visionary passion. His own nature—and the world's—doom him.

Ilbrahim, with his acute sensitivity and imaginativeness, is an infant miniature of the Romantic artist. He is gifted with the narrative faculty, and entertains his friend of a short season, a village boy receiving nursing in the Pearson home, with fanciful "romances."

As the boy became convalescent, Ilbrahim contrived games suitable to his situation, or amused him by a faculty which he had perhaps breathed in with the air of his barbaric birthplace. It was that of reciting imaginary adventures, on the spur of the moment, and apparently in inexhaustible succession. His tales were of course monstrous, disjointed, and without aim; but they were curious on account of a vein of human tenderness which ran through them all, and was like a sweet, familiar face, encountered in the midst of wild and unearthly scenery. The auditor paid much attention to these romances, and sometimes interrupted them by brief remarks upon the incidents, displaying shrewdness above his years, mingled with moral obliquity which grated very harshly against Ilbrahim's instinctive rectitude (I, 110-11) .

He is also possessed of the artist's penetrative power, although it fails him in the case of this boy, for Hawthorne tells us that "Ilbrahim was the unconscious possessor of much skill in physiognomy" (I, 110). And, young as he is, the "gentle boy" already betrays the artistic temperament of Romantic tradition:

> Ilbrahim would derive enjoyment from the most trifling events, and from every object about him; he seemed to discover rich treasures of happiness, by a faculty analogous to that of the witch hazel, which points to hidden gold where all is barren to the eye. . . . On the other hand, as the susceptibility of pleasure is also that of pain, the exuberant cheerfulness of the boy's prevailing temper sometimes yielded to moments of deep depression. His sorrows could not always be followed up to their original source, but most frequently they appeared to flow, though Ilbrahim was young to be sad for such a cause, from wounded love. The flightiness of his mirth rendered him often guilty of offences against the decorum of a Puritan household, and on these occasions he did not invariably escape rebuke. But the slightest word of real bitterness, which he was infallible in distinguishing from pretended anger, seemed to sink into his heart and poison all his enjoyments, till he became sensible that he was entirely forgiven. Of the malice which generally accompanies a superfluity of sensitiveness, Ilbrahim was altogether destitute; when trodden upon, he would not turn; when wounded, he could but die. His mind was wanting in the stamina for self-support; it was a plant that would twine beautifully round something stronger than itself, but if repulsed, or torn away, it had no choice but to wither on the ground (I, 108-9) .

It will be seen that this description might apply to Owen Warland, the idealistic artist of "The Artist of the Beautiful." Love blinds Ilbrahim, as it does Owen, for a little while, and he hopes to enjoy the love of the happy average. He seeks the affections of the young convalescent unexpectedly housed with him, a rough village boy who, like Peter Hovenden and his daughter, represents the understanding unillumined by imagination. Ilbrahim woos him with his "art," the tales born of his wild, "barbaric" nature, already mentioned. In just such a fashion, and just as hopelessly, will the twentieth-century artist-child, Tonio Kröger, in Mann's story, woo his commonplace Hans Hansen.

For Hawthorne has seen the empirical truth behind the romantic fable of the lonely child-genius: Ilbrahim foreshadows not only a theme of later fiction but the real childhood loneliness familiar to us in the biographies of modern artists. He is the boy Gide, who, he tells us in *Si le Grain ne Meurt*, came home from play one day able only to tell his mother, as he wept, *"Je ne suis pas pareil aux autres!"* Ilbrahim does not succeed in winning love and so escaping his doom. This "sweet infant of the skies that had strayed away from his home" (I, 97) is stoned by his playmates, "a brood of baby-fiends" (I, 112), and mocked and beaten by the one friend he had thought to have acquired. He perishes, the "victim of his own heavenly nature" (I, 113), a symbol of the tragic destiny of all those so endowed.

NOTES TO CHAPTER VIII

1 Emerson, writing in his Journal in 1851, saw no real difference in quality between the scientist's and the artist's "inspiration." "There is and must be a little air-chamber, a sort of tiny Bedlam in even the naturalist's or mathematician's brain who arrives at great results. They affect a sticking to facts; they repudiate all imagination and affection

as they would stealing. But Cuvier, Oken, Geoffroy-Hilaire, Owen, Agassiz, Audubon, must all have this spark of fanaticism for the generation of steam, and there must be that judicious tubing in their brain that is in the boiler of the locomotive" (*Journals of Ralph Waldo Emerson*, ed. E. W. Emerson and W. E. Forbes [Boston and New York: Houghton, Mifflin Co., 1909-14], VIII, 177) .

[2] Quoted in Stewart, *Nathaniel Hawthorne*, p. 82.

[3] *American Notebooks*, p. 106.

[4] Letters to Longfellow, June 4, 1837, and to Sophia Hawthorne, October 4, 1840 (Cowley, *Portable Hawthorne*, pp. 607-10; 611-13) .

[5] *American Notebooks*, p. xliv.

[6] "Hawthorne's Fanshawe: The Promise of Greatness," *New England Quarterly*, XXIII (1950) , 238 ff.

[7] See Eleanor M. Sickels, *The Gloomy Egoist* (New York: Columbia University Press, 1932) , pp. 305-6.

[8] *American Idealism* (Norman, Okla.: University of Oklahoma Press, 1943) , p. 64.

[9] Warren, *Nathaniel Hawthorne*, p. 367. As Warren indicates, the contradiction is clearly shown in two Notebook entries of Hawthorne's, made before writing the story: "A person to be in the possession of something as perfect as mortal man has a right to demand; he tries to make it better, and ruins it entirely" (1837) ; and "A person to be the death of his beloved in trying to raise her to more than mortal perfection; yet this should be a comfort to him for having aimed so highly and holily" (1840) .

[10] See *American Notebooks*, p. liii.

[11] *Wordsworth's Literary Criticism*, ed. N. C. Smith (London, H. Frowde, 1905) , p. 213.

[12] Letter to Nathaniel Hawthorne, March, 1851, in Thorp, *Herman Melville*, p. 387.

Chapter IX

Hawthorne the Artist

~~~~~~

One does not have to go back much further than the early nineteenth century to discover generations of artists entirely uninterested in their own careers as subject matter. Since then, and especially in our own times, we have become familiar with the artist-hero whose difficult relationship to life is the master problem of the author. Probably the modern theme of the artist's alienation—as we see it in Mann, in Gide, and in Joyce—is an outgrowth of the nineteenth-century myth of the artist as a special species—angel or demon, but not simply Man. The eighteenth century certainly did not find the poet either less or more than a whole man, and in the Renaissance poetry was a sign of manly competence.

Yet in our own time the theme of the artist's isolation has assumed a deeper seriousness than it held for the Romantics. The deified artist is gone altogether, and the gloomy splendor of Byronism has little to do with the shabby exile which the modern artist experiences. It is with this modern phase of the problem that Hawthorne, almost alone in his generation, seemed to be concerned. He saw the artist's isolation not as a becoming pose, but as the very real result of some new dislocation between the one and the many, the artist and the audience. He felt that the idealist philosophies which diverted his contemporaries widened this gap. This, surely, is one of the major themes of *The Blithedale Romance*, for when Coverdale suddenly resolves to return to the practical and material life of Boston, one cannot help feeling how absolutely right he is to do so, despite the superior goals of the Blithedalers. Coverdale, who may be closer to Hawthorne himself than any other of his characters, is the first outsider in American fiction, the man of high sensibility who finds himself alienated from the world and desperately sets out to capture the sense of it. The struggle against this alienation was a lifelong one for Hawthorne; he strove heroically for a sense of role and purpose for his art. He was not satisfied for it to be an activity on the margin of life, as it was for his Artist of the Beautiful, Owen Warland. Nor did he deem art worth the candle if its service meant a perverse and antihuman egotism, as he symbolically depicted it in "The Prophetic Pictures."

Certainly Hawthorne's own career shows an awareness of this problem that no one else, not even Melville, possessed. It is no longer customary to speak of Hawthorne as a recluse, ignorant of and indifferent to the "real world." Actually, he was probably closer to the gritty substance of American history than most of the cause-joiners of Concord. He was close to politics and politicians throughout his life, and he really knew better than most men what the odds were in his time against candor, idealism, and beauty. The desire which Hawthorne expressed in the Preface to *The Scarlet Letter*—"to live throughout the whole range of his faculties and sensibilities"—was, he must have found, doomed to frustration. For all the avenues leading into the real world increasingly disclosed a struggle dismayingly gross.

His college years, far from being a sheltered antechamber to the "outer" world, revealed immediately and exactly what the rest of life contained. His closest classmates, Pierce and Cilley and Morse, were already deep in the political maneuvering that was to occupy them all their lives—Cilley was to die in a rat-scrap duel brought to pass by political enmities. And Hawthorne himself may have worked for the Democrats; he was too honest and too unsparing of his own squeamishness to imagine that one could live in such an age and not be of it. One may well ponder why he always cleaved to these early friends—Pierce, Cilley, Morse, and Bridge—and eschewed the literary men and the philosophers. Young Henry Adams at Harvard was similarly to prefer the young Southerners he met to his own fine-boned breed, feeling something in them that was comfortingly uneccentric. They were the men of the norm.

Henry James thought that Hawthorne's constant struggle was that "between what may be called his evasive and his inquisitive tendencies."[1] He quoted from the famous 1837 letter to Longfellow: "Sometimes, through a peephole, I have caught a glimpse of the real world, and the two or three articles in which I have portrayed these glimpses please me better than the others." Perhaps it is more accurate to say that the statement is another indication of Hawthorne's suspicion that imaginative writing was leading him away from the main sources of everyday experience. And so, almost without any interruption during his entire writing life, Hawthorne kept those extraordinary notebooks of his explorations and observations of the actual. It is probably wrong to deplore their uninspired factuality—as James did—just as it is wrong to chastise the fiction Hawthorne wrote in the detached mode of allegory. What they tell us, rather, is that the sense of the mundane was always present in Hawthorne's mind and lay behind his more abstract imagining. We realize now that the "lonely chamber" to which he retired for the winning of fame was less a hermit's cave than a workshop to which he brought the gleanings of his long walking tours into rural New England.

His earliest tales are full of the results of this outgoing experience—despite the fact that their author himself was to charge them with being "flowers that blossomed in too retired a shade." That nevertheless he nearly failed to "open an intercourse with the world" was demonstration to him that the service of art was a questionable vocation which neither paid nor, possibly, deserved to pay.

He himself declared, in an oft-quoted passage, that

> he had no incitement to literary effort in a reasonable prospect of reputation or profit; nothing but the pleasure itself of composition,—an enjoyment not at all amiss in its way, and perhaps essential to the merit of the work in hand, but which, in the long run, will hardly keep the chill out of a writer's heart, or the numbness out of his fingers. To this total lack of sympathy, at the age when his mind would naturally have been most effervescent, the public owe it (and it is certainly an effect not to be regretted on either part), that the Author can show nothing for the thought and industry of that portion of his life, save the forty sketches, or thereabouts, included in these volumes (I, 13-14).

Poe had declared that the author of *Twice-Told Tales* was "the example *par excellence* in the country of the privately-admired and publicly unappreciated man of genius."[2] Even when the recognition arrived and Hawthorne became a classic in his own lifetime, the effect of these early years remained unforgotten. And whatever satisfactions he finally gave himself as a producing artist, the fact remained that he could never make a living by his writing. Long afterward he was to witness an insane actress burst into tears in an English poorhouse because of lack of attention, and to write:

> I appeal to the whole society of artists of the Beautiful, and the Imaginative,—poets, romancers, painters, sculptors,

actors,—whether or no this is a grief that may be felt even amid the torpor of a dissolving brain (VII, 50) .

In spite of the encouragement of men like Samuel Goodrich and Park Benjamin, and of anonymous publication in the annuals and monthlies, he found himself losing respect for himself as a valuable member of society. "I wish to God I could impart to you a little of my own brass," his friend Bridge wrote to him in 1837 as *Twice-Told Tales* went to press. "I have been trying to think what you are so miserable for. Although you have not much property, you have good health and powers of writing, which have made, and can still make, you independent."[3] But Hawthorne did lack the brass of his business friend. He was miserable, despite the healthy cast of his own nature, in the realization that his profession isolated him. He was prepared to be a critic of solitude, not only because he loathed its effects upon the solitary individual but because he longed for the world of steady purpose and happy labor, the rounded lives of the fishermen and farmers he met on his walks.

In the pathetic illusion that he, too, could enter that sort of life, he embraced the first of the many jobs which would keep him from his proper work; in 1839 he took up the duties of weigher at the Boston Custom House. Two years earlier, he had said to his sister: "I am tired of being an *ornament*. I want a little piece of land that I can call my own, big enough to stand upon, big enough to be buried in. I want to have something to do with this material world." He is said to have struck a nearby table as he spoke this, and to have added, "If I could only make tables I should feel myself more of a man." So it was natural that he should hope, rather fatuously, to find his identification with society in his workaday duties on the Boston docks, writing to Sophia as late as 1841:

But from henceforth forever I shall be entitled to call the

sons of toil my brethren, and I shall know how to sympathize
with them, seeing that I likewise have risen at the dawn, and
borne the fever of the midday sun, nor turned my heavy foot-
steps home-ward till eventide. Years hence, perhaps, the experience that my heart is acquiring now will flow out in truth
and wisdom.[4]

"It pleased thy husband," he wrote her, "to think that he
also had a part to act in the material and tangible business
of this life."

But in the end he was not able to convince himself of the
untruth that an artist, to know his fellow man, must labor
in another's furrow; he had his own work to justify by its
fruits. The familiar love letters to Sophia which were written from the Boston Custom House display a desperate
controversy which Hawthorne conducted with himself
upon the subject of art and its relation to the world of common things, of weighable things, like coal and salt. He
compelled himself to give his job his best attention (his
efficiency was commended) while he alternately praised his
education in reality and deplored "murdering so many of
the brightest hours of the day at that unblest Custom House,
that makes such havoc with my wits." He tried to convince
himself that there was superior moral worth in his thrall-
dom, or at least that his art would benefit from it in the
future. For Hawthorne, art was not its own justification;
all his life he would resolutely call upon himself to put his
writing aside for better-salaried work—chiefly because he
had to, but also (as has not generally been realized) because
he suspected the morality of self-absorbed artistic activity.

The same paradox characterized his reactions to his experience at Brook Farm. "What is the use of burning your
brains out in the sun when you can do anything better with
them?" his sister Louisa wrote.[5] Finally Hawthorne himself
acknowledged that his "life there was an unnatural and
unsuitable and unreal one," and asked, "Dost thou think it

a praiseworthy matter that I have spent five golden months in providing food for cows and horses?" And in the Salem Custom House he was still prey to the same doubts, imagining the disapprobation of his Puritan ancestors for the foolery of storytelling, and taxing himself for failing to see the spirit beneath the surface of his surroundings at the Custom House. Yet in 1847 he wrote to Longfellow:

> I am trying to resume my pen; but the influence of my situation and customary associates are so anti-literary, that I know not whether I shall succeed. Whenever I sit alone, or walk alone, I find myself dreaming about stories, as of old; but these forenoons in the Custom House undo all that the afternoons and evenings have done. I should be happier if I could write.[6]

The story was to be the same at the Liverpool consulate, the same to the end of his days. Hawthorne was never really to feel free, materially or morally, to devote himself entirely to that art for which his genius was designed.

We have noted the observation of Hawthorne's Oberon that the decision to devote oneself to the practice of art is perhaps dangerous anywhere, but certainly "fatal in New England" (II, 459), and his resolution to warn any would-be follower of his course against such a fate, and "as a text of deep and varied meaning, to remind him that he is an American" (XII, 30). Hawthorne remarked that in a man like Powers, with his mechanical ingenuity, "the set of his nature towards sculpture must indeed have been strong, to counteract, in an American, such a capacity for the contrivance of steam engines." The social meaning of "The Artist of the Beautiful" is, as we have noted, that in American society practical life was divorced from the creative impulse and unillumined by it. Hawthorne, then, was acutely aware that his America provided no honorable and necessary function for art. He was too much of a Puritan to regard with satisfaction a definition of art which made it a peripheral activity, neither honorable nor necessary.

It is for this reason, probably, that the expatriate mood seized him at the last. Though he spent barely seven years abroad, he felt the temptations of Europe more deeply than did Irving or Longfellow. His expatriation was the consequence of his experience of the division between practical and intellectual life in America, and consequently, it was an *inward* expatriation, such as James, and Whistler, and T. S. Eliot were to experience later, before they externalized it by residence abroad. If one wished to select any contemporary with whom Hawthorne shared this mood, one's choice would probably be Melville, who sought no solace in a foreign home but lived on, nearly to the end of the century, a forgotten exile in New York. Both Hawthorne and Melville felt that sense of unbalance between thought and action which American life was increasingly to enforce upon its artists, and which was to produce, beginning in the sixties and seventies, nostalgia for the older civilizations of Europe and nostalgia's actual result in physical transplantation. In anticipation of the impulse of these succeeding generations of artists, Hawthorne wrote, in Italy in 1858:

> It is very singular, the sad embrace with which Rome takes possession of the soul. Though we intend to return in a few months, and for a longer residence than this has been, yet we felt the city pulling at our heart strings far more than London did where we shall probably never spend much time again. It may be because the intellect finds a home there more than in any other spot in the world ... (X, 221).

And yet, he finally rejected the spurious comfort of expatriation:

> It would only be a kind of despair, however, that would ever

make me dream of finding a home in Italy; a sense that I had lost my country through absence or incongruity, and that earth, at any rate, is not an abiding place.

Nothing would be more misguided than an autopsy, at this remove, to discover the causes of the spiritual collapse that undoubtedly accompanied Hawthorne's physical disintegration in the last years of his life. Yet he seems to have faced some sort of crisis, the most serious kind that a creative artist can encounter, which resulted in the obstruction of his working power. Was he finally losing hold altogether of that sense of role for which he had battled for a lifetime? The posthumous novels bear witness to a paralyzing indecision, symbolized in the inability of his heroes to determine their allegiance to the present or to the past, to Europe or to America.

We have seen that Hawthorne's art is obsessed with the theme of guilt. One must ask why. Is it not simply that he would be an artist when every sign from man and Heaven indicated that the choice was a cursed one? How frequently in his work the artist is identified as an outcast, a vagabond —even perhaps a criminal! Is there a guilt-fantasy in the notebook jotting for a story to be based upon "an examination of wits and poets at a police-court and they to be sentenced by the judge to various penalties or fines"?[7] Much as one identifies one's other self in a dream, he seems to have seen himself in the image of the crippled North Adams soapmaker who told him, "My study is man . . .," and then, recognizing some kinship in Hawthorne, observed, "There is something of the hawkeye about you." Looking at his stump of a hand, the cripple added: "That hand could make the pen go fast." Did Hawthorne think of his own hand, that indeed could make the pen go fast, as having suffered some invisible mutilation?

NOTES TO CHAPTER IX

[1] James, *Hawthorne*, p. 54.

[2] Review of the second edition of *Twice-Told Tales, Graham's Magazine* (November, 1847) , reprinted in *The Shock of Recognition*, ed. Edmund Wilson (New York: Doubleday, Doran and Co., 1943) , p. 154.

[3] Horatio Bridge, *Personal Recollections of Nathaniel Hawthorne* (New York: Harper and Bros., 1893) , pp. 54, 73.

[4] Arvin, *Hawthorne*, p. 86.

[5] Julian Hawthorne, *Hawthorne and His Wife*, p. 232.

[6] Stewart, *Nathaniel Hawthorne*, p. 92.

[7] *American Notebooks*, p. 100.

Index